They said it couldn't be done,
but formally and legally . . .

GOD
OWNS MY
BUSINESS

GOD
OWNS MY
BUSINESS

STANLEY TAM

AS TOLD TO KEN ANDERSON

WINGSPREAD PUBLISHERS | CHICAGO

WingSpread Publishers
Chicago, Illinois

www.moodypublishers.com

An imprint of Moody Publishers

God Owns My Business New Edition
ISBN: 978-1-60066-340-6
LOC Catalog Card Number: 2007943303
© 1969, 2013 by R. Stanley Tam

Previously published by Christian Publications, Inc.
First Christian Publications edition 1969
First WingSpread Publishers edition 2012

Cover design by Erik M. Peterson
Cover illustration copyright © 2015 by Varijanta/iStock (492370788). All rights reserved.

We hope you enjoy this book from Moody Publishers. Our goal is to provide high-quality, thought-provoking books and products that connect truth to your real needs and challenges. For more information on other books and products written and produced from a biblical perspective, go to www.moodypublishers.com or write to:

Moody Publishers
820 N. LaSalle Boulevard
Chicago, IL 60610

3 5 7 9 10 8 6 4

Printed in the United States of America

*To
Juanita*

I wish to express my deep appreciation to Ken Anderson. I gave him a handful of "rough silver coins"—my personal experiences. With his God-given skill, he polished them into readable script. Then with his keen spiritual insight, he joined them together with his practical theology and preached to me a great sermon—"Nothing plus God equals God."

R. Stanley Tam

R. STANLEY TAM

In over 47 years of business life I have found
Christ to be the source of all my needs. Every
time He takes me through a valley He brings
me out stronger, wiser and more dependent
upon Him. My love and devotion for Him grow
each year. He gives me a purpose for which to live.

1

You cannot attach a more precarious tag to a man's name and reputation these days than to label him an outstanding Christian.

Disciples of our affluent image-making society promptly envision some kind of ecclesiastical oddity. Clergymen, to be sure, ought to be men of God. But for us laymen to seek the divine life is another matter. We should be dynamic in our communities. We should bolster the nation's economy. We should build and scheme and flex our muscles. We ought to attend church and contribute to its material needs. But we are not to be men who pray, men who take the Bible at face value, men who witness.

I realize this is the day of the hippy, the draft card burner, the rioter, disciples of the Hindu ashram, but these abnormals run in packs and in their conformity to faddist noncomformity escape the disdain encountered by standing alone.

What a sorry state we are in!

Well, if being serious about one's faith is a social error, I plead guilty, but with neither remorse nor apology. It is being thought of as an oddity that unnerves me. Not from a matter of personal pride, however. I'm upset about the whims of a society in which spiritual hunger and fulfillment seem to have become so abnormal.

Let me attempt an explanation.

My name is Stanley Tam. I'm a layman, a businessman. By many marketplace measurements I've succeeded in business. I like to sell, like to introduce new products, like to watch volume grow, like to make money. Recently the Dun and Bradstreet representative from our area went over our books and told me we had the most vigorous growth pattern of any comparable firm in our area. Right now I'm giving careful thought to another of a succession of expansion moves in our two corporations.

But although my business requires long hours at the office and constant surveillance and promotion, buying and selling is really no more than an avocation with me. My first concern is to succeed as a Christian. Let me state that a bit more definitely. My prime effort in life is to be obedient to my God, to serve Him and bring credit to His name.

Yet I insist I am not purposely trying to be a nonconformist. I'm not some overaged hippy, not an iconoclast, but a reasonably average human being.

Average?

Well, maybe I should strike that word from the record—not so much as it pertains to me but as it relates to God's potential for both you and me. For in the world as it is structured today, we should not settle for the spiritual plight of the average man.

I can understand the plight of being average in mentality or in physical endowments—because I surely qualify in both categories —but I do not understand why so many Christians read a Bible abounding in promises to make them something beyond themselves and yet settle for a spiritual vitality so mediocre as to seem virtually nonexistent. Consequently, the Christian who becomes demonstrably involved with God is looked upon as the rare exception far above the established rule.

On the contrary, it is my conviction God intended the full, rewarding life to be every person's birthright. We deny ourselves God's best for us by our own default, our impaired and often corroded sense of values. In God's sight, I am convinced, the oddity is the man who misses His mark for him, and the norm is the man who discovers the Christian life in all its dynamic perspective.

That's what Christianity is—the discovery of life!

No, even though obedience to God is my greatest concern, I do not consider myself an oddity. Nor am I trying to be different. I'm human, very much so, and I struggle to keep pride from blighting my Christian witness and perspective. Prejudices creep into my thought patterns and must be ferreted out. In the push of business I sometimes ask too much of my people and must apologize and make amends. My wife and four daughters could painfully document profuse evidences of stark humanity in my personal life. Though I try to make my Christian witness believable, as much of life as breath and heartbeat, some people have been known to cast reflections on my activities. Doubtless, at least in some cases, the impetus stems from a fault of my own.

But I believe tenaciously in the possibility of a man linking his life to God. I believe this to be the only truly good life, the kind of life within the grasp of every man, if he will simply and honestly endeavor to meet God's conditions.

Because of the unique way God has been pleased to bless this conviction, some rather unusual things have happened in my business. As a result, service clubs, churches, schools, and numerous other agencies all over North America permit me to address them giving testimony of God's intervention in my life. I have spoken to Jewish, Catholic, and Protestant groups. Monday and Tuesday may find me in the office, Wednesday at a banquet downstate; Thursday back in the office, Friday at a men's meeting in Omaha, the weekend in Portland or Seattle. Then back again for business the following Monday.

Often when the opportunity is given for me to share my story, other men experience a desire for spiritual involvement in their own lives. This is the psychology of life, eyeball-to-eyeball encounters with others. There is no better way to sell, no better way to communicate, to put ideas into motion.

Thus my motivation for recording this brief chronicle of my personal experiences—not so you can better understand Stanley Tam, but in the prayerful hope that encouragement and renewal will come to your own quest for the good and full life.

First, however, let me urge you not to use me as an example. I must live Stanley Tam's life, being obedient to the directives I feel God gives me, and you must live your life, being equally obedient to the priorities God asks of you. As feedback to my intimately pronounced intentions to obey Him, God has made what might be called singular demands upon my life. He may do the same to you or choose to orient and motivate you in completely different ways.

In my case I felt clearly directed by God literally to make Him my Senior Partner. At the outset this may seem naïve to you. If so, please hear me out. It's true. The stock in our two corporations is not owned by me or by members of our family; it is controlled by

3

a non-profit corporation whose sole purpose is to dispense funds for Christian work around the world. The only way my wife and I could regain control of the business would be to buy back the stock from that corporation.

But this was God's directive to us. He may lead you in an entirely different way. What's important is that you permit Him to show you His way, and when you see this way laid out before you, follow it in complete obedience. Obedience to God is the key to happiness and success in this life, our assurance of productive immortality.

2

We Tams are Scotch by extraction.

So the desire to make money probably entered my blood by genetic processes.

Great-grandfather McBeth, one of the stalwarts in my mother's lineage, emigrated from Scotland in 1849 when the whiff of gold sent men trampling over each other on the mad rush toward California. He apparently did well, for he eventually entered the banking business.

I was born just outside San Francisco, California, in 1915.

Grandfather Tam contributed no less to my heritage. Though perhaps not so adept in fiscal enterprises, he was a colorful individual. As a young man his eyes caught the glimmer of vaudeville lights, but since we Tams cannot lay claim to anything but ordinary physical prowess, he took up the art of legerdemain and actually became quite an accomplished magician. Vaudeville did not want for talent in those early days, however, and he gave far more performances in country schoolhouses than on the stage. My father served as his assistant.

Though he forsook magic in his later years, he kept a trunk full of tricks, and we children often succeeded in urging him to bring out his display and give us his rusty but nonetheless awesome artistry with the Chinese rings and now-you-see-it-now-you-don't bags and boxes of all sizes and descriptions.

In later years grandfather gave vent to his show business interests by teaming with my father in the purchase of several movie theaters, venturing as far away as Biloxi, Mississippi. Bright lights did not especially appeal to the son however, and on a vacation trip to Ohio he and my mother liked the looks of the Midwest and subsequently bought a farm in the Buckeye State.

I've lived in Ohio ever since.

We worked hard on the farm. One year we marketed five thousand bushels of potatoes and two thousand bushels of beans. Not bad for a 174 acre site that also pastured livestock and provided living space for the family.

Farming didn't appeal to me, particularly the hard manual labor involved. I did my bit. But I would sit by the hours mulling over get-rich-quick offers which came to our rural mailbox so often in those days. When I could afford the price of postage, I clipped coupons and sent in for free samples and information, making the daily arrival of the mail carrier a gala event. And what a wonderful array it was. Garden seeds. Candy samples. Automotive lubricants. Kitchen extracts. Surefire potions for gaining or losing weight. Cream to remove freckles. Greasy stuff to glamorize the hair. The manly art of self-defense. Secrets of ventriloquism. Mesmerism. Finding buried treasure. Insuring long life.

With many of these samples came sales programs virtually guaranteed to make one independent overnight. I wanted to try my hand at selling, but congenital shyness held me back. How could I ever hope to muster sufficient courage? I dreamed of becoming a salesman. I wanted to make something of myself, but the grit to start just wasn't in me.

But I did have initiative, and I expended it on odd jobs of every description. If I saw a neighbor's house needing improvement, I would suggest it and offer myself as the solution. I painted mailboxes, mended fences, washed windows, mowed lawns.

Then one day in a moment of gumption I clipped a coupon, mailed it to the firm involved, and subsequently found myself set up with a display case for door-to-door peddling of household items.

It was painful.

But I slowly built confidence, could take refusals in stride, and began polishing the technique of turning a sale. Business did not boom in proportion to the adjectives in the advertisements, but it wasn't long until I needed the assistance of two fellow schoolmates as auxiliary salesmen. John D. Rockefeller, the tycoon of that era,

6

could not have felt more self-assured than I, as I tabulated my inventory and sales by the light of a kerosene lamp.

My penchant for selling continues to be enigmatic to me since my nature tends toward reticence. Looking back upon my childhood I see a rather nice but terribly backward little boy who invariably ran from a fight, cried easily, took a negative attitude to things.

Girls fascinated and frightened me. Schoolroom romances consisted largely of passing notes, but I was so spineless that when I finally determined to express my sentiments to a little brunette I did so by having another girl expedite the communication for me.

We lived a short distance from a shantytown community, and I dreaded going near the place. But I had to pass through it enroute to town, and often local bullies would cow me into a corner and half-scare the hope of life out of me. When we had some extra Saturday money, a friend and I would go in for treats, running like gazelles through the tough community. Sometimes we would be apprehended, however, and asked to turn over our money. I always complied without so much as token resistance.

I hated myself for being such a coward and often fell asleep at night imagining I had answered one of the muscle-builder magazine advertisements and had suddenly come into such virility that the boys of the neighborhood shrunk into the shadows at the sight of me.

But I always awakened to reality.

Though, as previously indicated, our family had colorful backgrounds, my home demonstrated little of the bliss a child needs. Quarreling was commonplace. I had a pet pig, my pride and joy raised as a 4-H project, and I kept the animal and his pen spotlessly clean. More than once I fled the din of the domicile to curl up for the night beside my four-footed friend.

My shyness and the lack of affection to bulwark my personality weakness drove me into deeper introversion. I spent hours alone, sometimes idling back and forth along the fields, dreaming of the future. The more I dreamed, the more I knew I would be a salesman. True, my shyness gave me a lot of difficult moments. A gruff customer could send me scurrying to the street, frightened at the thought of ever again ringing another strange doorbell, but I always summoned courage to go after another sale.

Like any introvert, I had moments of normal confidence such as in the home of a cordial customer and when making a sale. Friends and schoolteachers also gave me encouragement. Life had many bright moments.

The Boy Scouts provided a positive outlet for me all the way through high school. By this time the Depression had taken full grip upon the nation's economy, and money for anything other than the bare essentials did not come easily.

So I went to the scoutmaster one day and said, "Why don't we make some money for the troop?"

"How, Stan?"

"Well, I know a company that sets you up in stuff like kitchen extracts. Each of the guys could sell to women around his house and people he knows, and we'd put the profits in the treasury."

"Sounds like a good idea," the leader responded. At the age of seventeen I had been named his assistant, and he put a lot of confidence in me, one of the strongly contributing factors to my determination to make good.

We gave it a try.

But the other scouts quickly lost interest, and I ended up buying the wares and selling them myself.

As I said, the depression was in full sway, and though my parents struggled valiantly to keep the farm solvent, they failed. Like so many agrarians, they lost the farm through foreclosure.

It was a shattering blow.

In 1933 we moved into Lima.

Though I had done fairly well in high school, college was out of the question. I did take a correspondence course in salesmanship, but that was to be the sum of my higher education. Things were rough, and I knew I had to make it on my own.

My parents tried to give me encouragement. We had a lot of strife in our home, true, but my parents emphasized good character, clean habits, and dependability. I forgive them for the darker moments, because it was rough for them, and they did not have spiritual resources to fall back upon. We attended a little country church, both Sunday school and worship. Though my parents professed nothing of a vital faith in God, they wanted us children to develop strong moorings.

They expressed pride in my initiative, and this gave me sorely needed encouragement.

One day I sent away for a book on formulae, another of the prosperity incentives which came to my attention, and one of the concoctions showed how to reclaim waste oil. Thus began the Tam-o-shanter Oil Company, producers of penetrating oil which I both manufactured and sold.

With fifteen dollars saved from my enterprise, I became the first boy in the neighborhood to own a Model T car. It bolstered my ego and helped boom my business. Not only did I continue selling projects, but with such fine transportation, I could now pick up scrap metal, paper, old clothes, and sundry items.

I subsequently owned two more Model T's. It was good, driving down the countryside, watching people turn their heads to see the successful Tam boy chugging by.

One of those cars was to be part of the many thrilling chapters the Lord has permitted me to have. Though not an expert mechanic I liked to putter with engines, and I decided to turn a little profit by sprucing up this car and offering it for sale.

A clothing salesman answered my newspaper ad, offering to pay the eighteen dollars I asked. He gave me a five dollar down payment and I, yet unseasoned in business procedures, yielded to his insistence that I turn the title over to him.

He never paid me another cent.

I will tell you the end of that story later—a story which was to take thirty years for completion—but first I want you to know how the negatives in my life turned to positive, how God became vital to me, and how faith in Him became the premise for all my activity.

3

We kept milk cows back on the farm, and it usually fell the lot of my sister and me to milk them, a chore neither of us relished. Consequently, it was usually quite late in the day before I summoned the gumption to go out after them.

On one such evening—at the age of ten, as I recall—dusk had fully gathered by the time I footed my way to the last of the herd and sent them lowing toward the barn.

A full moon rose, big like the balloons used for manned ascensions at the county fair. I stopped in my tracks, caught by its beauty. From the time the Psalmist David looked in awe at the skies, and probably long before that, man has had his thoughts turned to God at the sight of celestial bodies. So it was with me that night.

"Who are you, God?" I whispered. "I would like to know you."

It was a simple utterance, hardly classifiable as a prayer, but it gave evidence of spiritual hunger. The hunger had been voiced for the first time, and I have had many subsequent reasons to believe God heard those words and deigned to answer them.

Yet many years passed without any overt action on my part toward faith in God. Observing me you might have said I was like the general run of youth in the age of life when spiritual matters are apparently of no importance. I outgrew Sunday school, though I did attend church, and developed something of an aversion to what we called church people, particularly those who felt it their responsibility to waft the aroma of fire and brimstone under the nostrils of the wayward and the uncommitted.

One day as my cousin Bud and I drove down the street in my Model T, we came alongside his aunt returning from the store.

"Let's give her a ride," Bud said.

So I pulled up to the curb.

"Hop in. Me an' Stan'll take you home."

She looked at us with apprehension, her face taut, her eyes cold as stone.

"Stan's a careful driver," Bud prodded. "Get on in. All them groceries y'got are too heavy to carry."

Bud helped her in. I glanced at them, and she gave me an acid look as though I had done something wrong.

"Okay," Bud called out when they were both seated again, "let 'er rip!"

I floored the clutch pedal, slowly released the brake, and pulled down the throttle lever on the steering bar. The well-tuned engine responded, plunging us forward in an enormous surge of power for those early days of automotive engineering.

"Take it easy there, young fellow!" Bud's aunt called out.

Bud looked at me and grinned. "You're scarin' the gall stones outa her," he mumbled. "Give it the gas!"

We chugged forward, mildly careening around a sharp turn, heading for the woman's house. But to even the faintest of hearts the piddling speed of a Model T quickly became commonplace, and so she gradually regained composure.

"What kind of devilment are you boys up to?" she wanted to know. "Why are you gallavantin' around like this?"

"We ain't up to nothin' at all," Bud told her. "We was just drivin'—"

"The Lord help us," she broke in. "I don't know what things is a commin' to. Young people runnin' off to dances, playin' cards, goin' to the movies. Like as not you two was just at the pool room, wasn't you?"

"No, Auntie. Like I said—"

"You're both on the road straight to hell! We're havin' a prayer meeting at the church tonight. If you was to use an ounce of sense, the both of you, you'd be there and get converted."

When we drove away from her house, I turned to my cousin and said, "Look, Bud, let's not ever pick her up again."

"Aw, she means right."

"She sure doesn't know how to sell."

"What d'ya mean, Stan?"

"If I was to approach my customers the way she does, just talk about price instead of building up the product, I wouldn't turn a nickle all day long."

The comment was intended to be casual, spoken and then forgotten. Looking back, however, I suspect I said what I did about Bud's aunt because of the unvoiced spiritual hungers latent in my thoughts. I have never aspired to fame or greatness, but I had a consuming desire to make something of myself, and even then I must have at least suspected how important faith in God could be as a guide on the road to success.

A few weeks later I drove up to a farm home, grasped my display case, and headed for the door. Selling had been getting real tough because money was extremely tight, and I had to face a lot of resistance. A woman might open the door a crack, curious to know what you had to sell or if you had samples to give away, but then would give all kinds of excuses for not letting you in.

As a matter of technique on farm-to-farm calls, I took note of the name on the mailbox. It was helpful to be able to address a woman by her last name. Occasionally, of course, the name would be incorrect, and I would lose instead of gain.

On this particular morning the name on the mail box was George Long. The lawn was well-mowed. A bed of flowers blossomed near the veranda. So I was prepared to say, "Good morning, Mrs. Long. I'm curious about the name of those beautiful flowers you have growing over there."

To my surprise the door did not come open a peep in response to my knock. It opened wide, revealing a most pleasant woman who looked at me as though she had been waiting since daybreak for me to come with my display of merchandise.

"M-Mrs. Long?" I stammered, forgetting all about the flowers.

"That's right," she replied. "I'm so glad to see you. Won't you please come in?"

"Well, yes, I will as a matter of fact," I said, "if you don't mind."

Moving ahead of me, she gestured to a chair by the table. I went to it, sat down, and swept my eyes across the room in search for any clue to her enthusiasm. A large Bible lay on the table. Two wall mottos displayed Bible verses.

My thoughts went back to Bud's aunt. But I didn't cringe. This Mrs. Long was a far cry from the woman who rode in my Model T and proclaimed my benightedness.

"I take it you're a salesman," she primed.

"Yes, that's right, Ma'am."

I opened my case and laid out samples of the wares I had to offer. She listened intently, encouraging me to something more than my usual marketing eloquence.

"Well," she said when I finished, "money is scarce as can be. You know that. It keeps a body figuring to put food on the table."

My spirits ebbed.

"However," she continued, "I will take a couple of things. You made an excellent presentation. You have a lot of talent."

"Well, thank you, Mrs. Long!" I exuded.

We completed the transaction.

Then I said, "We don't need to worry about money much longer. President Roosevelt has a great program going. He'll have us out of this depression in a few months."

"You think so?"

"I'm sure of it. Take his NRA program, for example."

This led us into a political discussion which centered for the most part around Mrs. Long's concern over motivations in our country. She wasn't a diehard reactionary by any means, but she felt men were looking in the wrong direction for the answers to their problems.

I grew uneasy, got up to go.

"Just a moment," Mrs. Long said. "Please sit down."

I sat.

"I gave you time to tell me about the things you have to sell," she continued. "Now maybe you would be willing to listen to my presentation."

So it was to be a case of bartering. She had lifted my spirits by making a cash purchase, but now she wanted the money back for some item she had to offer.

"Like I said," she went on, "you are a talented young man. You'll make your mark in this world. I wish you well. But no matter how successful you become, even if you acquire a great deal of wealth, you'll always be striving for something more. You'll never be satisfied. Never. Not until you settle the most important of all questions in life."

"What is that?" I asked.

She smiled. "Your relationship to God."

"Oh," I countered, "I attend church. I suppose you might say I'm a little bit unusual in that I have no bad habits. I don't smoke or drink. I don't even use profanity."

"Do you know Jesus Christ?" Mrs. Long asked.

It was not a theological question, not a trace of tirade, but the warm interrogation of a person who seemed sincerely anxious to help me.

"Do you?"

"Well, uh," I stammered, "I. . . ."

The words logjammed on my tongue.

For the next two hours I listened as this woman told me what Jesus Christ meant to her. She told me how empty her life had been, how she had tried to find satisfaction, to discover the sense of living. Nothing quite added up until her personal encounter with the Son of God.

I'll tell you something: Mrs. Long could sell! She believed in the product! She had experienced its benefits!

She told me of answers to prayer in her life. She told me of being able to talk to God as one talks to a friend. She told me how she had prayed that her house might become a sanctuary for people seeking spiritual guidance. (I later learned I was the seventh person to come in answer to that prayer. Many more were to follow.)

Just as the time came when she would normally have invited me to receive Christ into my life, a carload of relatives drove into her yard. I excused myself and left.

Even though I wanted to get away from her as fast as I could, I left her home reluctantly. This kind of person was supposed to be a religious fanatic in my glossary of definitions. But not Mrs. Long. She was radiant and genuine, compelling without offensive pressure. I was convinced she had spiritual reality, and this was what I wanted.

Driving away from her farm that morning, I tried to pray, tried to make a deal with God, to come to terms with Him. Of course, I wanted those terms to be my terms, compatible to my ideas, my prejudices, my self-esteem.

This remarkable woman had told me one must confess his basic sinfulness, his total inadequacy to generate valid righteousness. But that would strip me of pride, of my slowly growing sense of personal confidence, of being able to take care of myself.

My cousin Bud and I had been attending church with some degree of regularity, both Sunday morning and evening. Attending church was routine in our area for decent people, but I had a take-it-or-leave-it attitude. Now I seemed to hear Mrs. Long's words in the sermons, the songs, the prayers. The church was what might be called old-line, giving emphasis on worship Sunday mornings and evangelism Sunday night. Evangelism included a call for sinners to come to the altar and make public their renunciation of the old life and acceptance of the new. I was intrigued as seekers responded to the Sunday night invitation.

Some wept in repentance, then wept for joy. Others gave forthright witness of the transformation that had taken place in their lives. It confused me. Suppose I went to the altar? Would this be my experience? Did I want it to be?

"What do you suppose happens, Bud?" I asked. "The way some of those people act when they get converted—it's like they got hit with an electric shock or something."

"I guess it's different with different people," Bud philosophized. "Like at a ball game. One guy yells his tonsils loose while somebody else sits there like it was a checker game or somethin'. They're both just as interested in the game."

"Maybe the second fellow gets more out of it than the first," I suggested.

"Could be," Bud agreed.

"How about you, Bud?"

"Me?"

"You figure to get converted someday?"

"Yeah, someday."

"Any idea when?"

"Nope. How about you?"

I shrugged my shoulders.

At times I wanted to give up the idea. But I couldn't. There was this impelling urge in my heart. There was the memory of the morning at Mrs. Long's house.

"So many people have Christianity all confused," she had told me. "Some of them think it's a lot of 'do this' and 'don't do that.' Others try to work it out for themselves. Stanley, all you do to become a Christian is to just let God make you a changed person.

In ourselves we can't attain salvation any more than we could give ourselves physical life. God must do it for us, but He can't unless we let Him."

One Saturday night Bud and I walked the streets of Lima as was the custom. This was the boy-meets-girl parade. A pretty girl often turned my head, but this time my thoughts were a million miles away from romantic inclinations.

"Bud," I said, "I've been doing a lot of thinking."

"Yeah? What about?"

"About religion. You know, the way they preach it at church."

Bud was quiet.

"Don't you ever think about it?"

"Sure I do."

We walked on half a block or so, neither of us speaking.

"You still haven't decided when you plan to give in?"

"Nope. I sure aim to, though."

"But you've got to do more than just aim to."

"I guess so, Stan."

We stopped for a malt. We were alone and could talk.

"I don't know about you, Bud," I said, "but tomorrow night at church I'm going to get this salvation business settled."

"Y'are?" Bud looked at me in a kind of wonderment.

"I want you to help me."

"Well, say now, I'm not sure if I can do that."

"Sure you can."

"How?"

"I want us to sit together in church like we always do, only I want to sit on the aisle with you next to me. Then when the preacher gives the altar call for sinners to come forward I want you to give me a good shove."

"You want me to do what?" Bud exclaimed.

"Shove me out into the aisle. If you'll just give me a start, I think I can make it the rest of the way down to the altar."

Sunday morning dawned in singular beauty. I went to Sunday school, attended the morning worship, but heard little of what was said. My thoughts had zeroed onto the forthcoming evangelistic meeting. Did I really want to go through with it? Would I have the courage to go to the altar?

I took a long walk that afternoon.

Why did I have to make a public display of myself? Why

couldn't I simply tell God I recognized my need, my sins, and then ask Him to make this salvation business happen? Why couldn't I do it right now as I walked?

It seemed pointless to question, for in those days conversion related directly to the altar rail, at least in our community, and to claim salvation apart from the altar route might be considered heterodoxical. In any case, I felt my conversion, if it occurred, must transpire at the altar. And perhaps this was as it should have been, the summoning of my fullest supply of courage to make a public commitment.

As the hour neared for the evening service, conflicting emotions tormented my mind. At times I anticipated, at times I dreaded, but one thing was sure—I must attend that service.

Bud and I arrived just before the pastor announced the first hymn. We sat near the back, I on the aisle, my cousin directly beside me.

I'd be at a loss to try to tell you what the preacher talked about that night. It hardly seemed as though I was in a church building. It was more like suspended animation. I had the feeling the preacher singled me out the way a hunter does his target in a flock of geese.

It was miserable.

Yet assuring.

For God was bringing into fruition the simple prayer of that ten-year-old who looked into the rising glow of the moon and whispered, "Who are you, God? I would like to know you."

God is God. What a vitalizing thought! He loves us and wants us to come to know and to love Him. He may lead over variant circumstances, but He will lead any person who sincerely seeks to find Him.

The sermon concluded.

I looked at my hands. They were trembling. My heart pounded. I breathed as though I had been running.

With gentle persuasion the pastor now spoke to those in the audience who recognized their spiritual need and now deliberated whether or not they would take the step of faith to meet this need. Kindness permeated his words. I had the strong feeling he cared about such as me, wanted to help, wanted to be a guide through the strange path of affirmed decision.

The audience stood to sing the hymn of invitation. Without waiting for the agreed upon boost from Bud, I stepped into the aisle and strode resolutely to the front of the sanctuary. There I knelt at the altar.

Others came; quite a number.

A counselor knelt beside me, and, taking me step by step through the pages of the New Testament, showed me God's plan for personal salvation just as Mrs. Long had done. *All have sinned and come short of the glory of God. . . . Christ died for our sins. . . . Whosoever shall call upon the name of the Lord shall be saved.*

"Talk to the Lord," the counselor said, "as you talk to me. In your own words, Stanley, tell Him you recognize your need and are willing to let Him meet that need."

I closed my eyes, bowed my head.

"God," I prayed. "I'm a sinner. I can't earn my own salvation. That's why you sent Jesus to the world, to make it possible for me to have salvation. I accept Jesus right now as my personal Savior."

I lifted my head, slowly opened my eyes.

"God bless you, Stanley," the counselor said. "Did you mean that prayer?" he asked.

I nodded.

"Well, what does the Scripture say?" He again opened his Bible to the book of Romans, pointed to a verse.

"Whosoever shall call upon the name of the Lord," I read quickly.

"You called?"

"Yes."

"Then what has happened to you?"

"I. . . ."

"God says to call upon Him. You called, didn't you?"

"Yes, I did."

"Did you mean it when you told the Lord you were accepting Him into your life?"

"Yes, sir, I did."

"Don't you believe the Lord heard that prayer?"

"I sure hope so."

"It's more than hoping so, Stanley," the counselor said kindly. "God plainly says if we call He will answer. Assurance is in His word, not in our hopes or feelings. God doesn't lie. If you keep your part of the bargain, He will keep His part. Do you believe that?"

"Yes, sir."

"Then what happened when you called upon Him just now?"

"He . . . He heard me."

"And so what have you become?"

"I. . . ."

"If from a sincere heart you called upon the Lord, asking Him to save you from your sins, what has happened?"

"I've become a Christian."

"You surely have!" he exclaimed.

He extended his hand. I offered mine. He grasped my hand warmly, and we shook.

I looked now at others around the altar of prayer. Many wept. Some radiated happiness at the realization of conversion. Both of these emotions had bypassed me.

I was troubled.

Doubts came deeply and darkly into my heart.

4

It is good to have honest doubts.

The Bible tells us to *prove all things; hold fast to that which is good.* The genuine conversion experience involves an enormous vault from the finite to the infinite, during which time the convert remains essentially the same person he was before. If he was impatient, he remains impatient. If he had a quick temper, he doesn't suddenly overcome it. Whatever his personality weaknesses, he retains them.

But there is one tremendous difference.

Through the presence of the Holy Spirit, Christ begins a process of change. *If any man be in Christ,* the Bible assures us, *he is a new creature. Old things are passed away. Behold, all things are become new.*

A man begins building on a new foundation.

Jesus Christ.

But the Bible also tells us to *grow in grace and in the knowledge of our Lord and Savior Jesus Christ.*

We have a foundation.

We build upon that foundation.

It's a wonderful, transforming experience! It begins in a moment and lasts for a lifetime!

True, my Christian faith has never been what you would call an emotional experience. My preference is to look at a proposition squarely, analyze it, put it to the test, believe what I see to be true, and reject what I find to be untrue. God dealt with me on this basis. He makes no two people alike. And I suspect a lot of folks get into religious maladjustment because they think faith is a synonymn for conformity, not realizing that—whereas faith in Christ makes us eligible for the most rewarding of all human fellowship—God never intended to make any two Christians exactly alike.

I did have initial doubts.

It bothered me—the sameness in my personality during those post-conversion days. Yet I knew something had happened. I had taken God at His word. The Bible pointed an unwavering finger at my need, proclaimed the redemption made possible through Christ's life and death and resurrection, and assured me that simply by committing my life to Christ in an act of childlike faith I had become a son of God.

The Bible holds the key!

I will always remember the words of the counselor who helped me come to the point of decision at the church altar. "Assurance is in God's Word, not in our hopes or feelings." This is the whole purpose of the Bible—to state God's conditions and provisions, not only for the beginning of the life in Christ but also for the continuity of this life.

Very frankly as I have indicated, the earliest moments of my Christian experience involved uncertainty and frustration, but as I began studying the Bible these doubts dissipated and the solidity of faith took their place.

But only the Word of God can lead us into this assurance and progressive maturity.

Participation in church activities should play an important role in every Christian's life. Many times a good sermon has stimulated me to higher spiritual aspirations. I'm old-fashioned enough to believe adults should attend Sunday school. But until a man learns how to get along with the Bible, how to dig into its inexhaustible treasures for inspiration and counsel and guidance, he cannot hope to experience spiritual maturity.

Now, of course, I'm aware of the maelstrom of argument surrounding the Bible these days. Is it the Word of God or does it merely contain the Word of God? Has it become at best some kind of historical record of man's relentless search for meaning beyond himself? Frankly, I have neither the time nor the scholarly background to participate in the discussion. By this I do not mean to say there is no place for honest debate, that we must blindly cling to dogma even though reason may be at complete odds with that dogma. If the Bible is the living Word of God, it is equal to whatever test of accuracy men may feel inclined to give it.

All I can say—and this I say with resounding certainty—is that from the outset of my conversion, the Bible became my constant guide and companion. Through the years I have made a practice of rising before the rest of the family in order to be able to spend a half-hour to an hour, and sometimes more, reading my Bible and permitting its truths to permeate my thinking.

The Bible tells us *faith comes by hearing, and hearing by the Word of God.* In simple language this means you cannot generate or conjure or philosophize the Christian faith. This faith comes from only one source—the Word of God.

I'm convinced a lot of argument over the validity of the Scriptures would evaporate if men would come to the Bible in humility, realizing their need of divine light, recognizing the Bible as a lamp unto our feet and a light unto our path, and let God convict and cleanse and motivate through His Word.

Pardon me if I seem to transgress theological grounds in saying this, but I suspect God purposely made it difficult for the intellectual mind to accept the Bible as His inspired book. The crossing of the Red Sea, the experiences of Jonah, the miracles of the New Testament—all of these have a disciplinary effect upon the quest for faith, compelling us to come to God in humble, childlike wonder, recognizing that He is God and that nothing is impossible for Him.

But let us leave theological controversy for others. Instead I want to suggest to you a function of Bible exploration which has been of utmost significance to me.

It is important to read and study the Bible. But one can do this and still miss the real reason God gave this record of His mind and heart to us. The key to unlocking the inspiration held in the boundless reservoir of the Bible's pages is meditation. I often spend an hour on one verse of the Bible, possibly one phrase or one word. I ask God to make the meaning clear to me—not the theological meaning or the doctrinal meaning but the relevance of this nugget of truth to my own life. What does it say in terms of guidance? Does it point out a weakness in my personality which needs to be corrected? Is it a window showing me the greatness of my Lord in a display of magnitude I have not seen before?

22

In meditation the Bible amplifies its significance to the Christian. Through meditation the Book becomes intimately relevant. So, God's Word not only provided firm ground on which to plant my faith, but I began to sense heartening changes in my life.

My negative attitude took a positive trend. I became more outgoing, more poised, more aware of the purpose of life. The promises contained in the Bible became a part of my frame of reference. *No good thing will He withhold from them that walk uprightly. Call upon me and I will show you great and mighty things. My God shall supply all your needs, according to His riches in glory by Christ Jesus.* Nugget promises such as these challenged me to prove for myself that God does indeed wish not only to intercept our paths but also to walk beside us on those paths.

I began to trust God for simple things . . . to help me start my car on cold mornings . . . to lead me to sales contacts . . . to show me how both to make ends meet and at the same time slowly expand my marketing potential By this time I had begun my earliest exploitations of the silver business and the vicissitudes involved tested the tensile strength of my new faith. Only by using faith are we kept from losing it, and to use faith is to lose the unbelief which so often hinders God's intervention in the lives of His children.

My faith was to be put to use as I struggled to learn the art of walking with God daily On one sales trip down in Ohio and Kentucky, things went poorly for me. I decided to head home. After filling up with gas in Athens, Ohio, I had seventy-eight cents left. Discouraged, I drove out onto the highway, grateful that I had sufficient fuel to make it back to Lima.

Ten miles down the road my motor became noisy. Obviously, a rod was about to burn out. Slowing to a crawl, I nursed the engine into a small town up ahead and stopped at a garage on the outskirts.

"Yep," said the proprietor, "y'got a rod burnt. I ain't too busy this mornin' so I'll fix it for ya."

"How much?" I asked fearfully.

"Oh, let's see now."

He looked at the motor puckered his lips. He was friendly enough but obviously not given to charity when it came to figuring a price.

"Ten bucks sound fair enough?"

My heart sank.

Please God, I prayed silently, *what am I going to do? I don't have ten dollars.*

"Little short of cash?" the man asked.

I nodded.

"Where d'ya live?"

"Lima."

He shook his head. "Nope," he said, "can't give credit that far away. You may be as honest as a preacher, but to tell ya the truth I had a preacher skip out owin' me a good sum once."

My God shall supply all your needs!

The promise, fruition of my dependence upon the Bible as the source of faith, came to my thoughts. I claimed it in silent affirmation and in my heart came a whispered assurance that somehow God would meet my need.

He did!

"How much money y'got?" the mechanic asked.

I told him.

He had obviously thought he might work some deal, but my financial straits were far too stringent. Looking at me half pitying, half disgusted, he turned and began walking away.

Please God! I prayed.

Suddenly the man turned. Pointing, he said, "See that high school on the hill? They've got a mechanics class up there that works on cars an' don't cost a thing. Little rough on my business for a time till folks saw these boys can't be expected to be dependable, but they'd fix your lizzy good 'nough to make it to Lima, I'd reckon."

In a few hours I was headed for home once more.

I remember coming into a store one morning, desperately in need of making a sale, and placing my display on the counter. The proprietor seemed to like what he saw, and for a moment I thought he would sign.

Then abruptly he said, "No," and assumed the air of wanting me to leave as quickly as possible.

I was keenly disappointed. I dealt exclusively with photographers and X-ray labs, which meant only a few sales prospects in any given town, and this shop was something of a last hope. Yet, though I needed business, an assuring peace came to my heart. God knew my needs. He had not forgotten me. *All things work together for good to them that love God* is His promise.

So I smiled, bid the man good day, and turned to leave.

"Wait a minute, young man!" he called out.

I hesitated at the door.

"Come back here," he said.

I returned to the counter.

"I get a little tired of salesmen," he said. "They butter you all up, an' if you don't buy they act like snakes. I've about had my fill of it. To tell you the truth I sort of liked that idea of yours, but I got this bellyful attitude about salesmen. Only there's something different about you. Something real different."

He became one of my steady customers!

In conjunction with my work of stopping at photo studios, I struck onto the sideline of picking up outdated negatives. When you have your picture taken, the photographer files the negative, hoping for repeat business. After five years or so, however, he presumes you are no longer interested and discards the file. I took to picking up these old negatives, taking them to a firm in Valparaiso, Indiana, that had a process whereby they washed off the gelatin emulsion, leaving the celluloid which could be cut into squares and sold to billfold manufacturers as identification covers.

It provided a good sideline for my sales forays, often covering gas and oil.

On another of those occasions when I had run precariously low on cash, I routed myself homeward on U. S. 30 so I could stop in Valparaiso with some eighty dollars worth of old negatives, no trivial amount in those days.

Arriving at the reclamation plant, I took my salvage to the warehouse, got a slip, and went to the office for my money.

"We'll send it to you," the girl said.

"I'd like to have it now," I told her.

"I'm sorry. The boss is out of town today, and there's nobody here to sign the check."

"Look," I exclaimed, "I'm broke!"

"That's too bad," she said with very little sympathy in her voice.

I waited a moment. She returned to her work. I went outside.

Actually, I wasn't dead broke. I had about two gallons of gas in the car and exactly thirteen cents in my pocket. Lima was some one hundred and eighty miles on down the road. I could leave the car, hitchhike home, but that would mean coming all the way back when I got the money.

I breathed a prayer asking God for guidance.

Feeling impressed to start for home, I got into the car, drove a couple of blocks, then glanced at the faltering gas gauge. It seemed pointless to drive farther. So pulling off to the side, I bowed my head over the steering wheel and prayed again.

Once more came the strong conviction to keep driving.

"But, Lord," I reasoned, "There's only two gallons of gas in the tank and thirteen cents in my pocket.

The conviction remained.

There was a hamburger shop across the street. This was the era of the nickle burger. So I decided to get some nourishment. After one hamburger and a glass of water I had eight cents left.

Somewhat reluctantly I drove into a filling station.

"Look," I hedged, "you, uh, wouldn't sell me eight cents worth of gas, would you?"

The attendant looked at me curiously, probably supposing I had been drinking.

"Eight cents is all I've got," I said, hoping he might offer to extend credit.

"Well," he drawled, "if that's all you've got, then I s'pose that's all I can sell you."

He took the nozzle off the pump, inserted it into my tank, and gave me exactly eight cents worth. To the drop.

Heavy darkness had fallen by the time I drove a short distance. I kept working on a formula in my mind to determine when the fuel would be exhausted, wondering if I ought to stop, and yet urged on by the conviction which had followed my prayers for guidance.

Around a turn in the road my headlights picked up the form of a chap about my age thumbing a ride.

I never picked up hitchhikers. My father had been robbed by vagrants. Newspapers carried several stories telling of people murdered by those they had picked up. So I had decided not to expose myself to this kind of danger.

By a strange compulsion, however, I veered off the road and braked to a stop just ahead of the hiker.

"Hey, fella," he exclaimed, as he scooted in beside me, "thanks for stopping! A farmer dropped me off here in the middle of nowhere a couple of hours ago, and I'd about given up trying to hail a car. I thought sure I'd have to hoof it to the next town."

I shifted carefully into low, slowly let out the clutch, cautiously pressed the accelerator. I was determined to get every possible bit of yardage out of the skimpy fuel supply.

"How far are you going?" my new companion asked.

"I'm not sure," I replied. My eyes drifted to the gas gauge. "How far are you going?"

"I live in Marion, Ohio," he said.

"That's just beyond Lima."

"Right. You going that far?"

"I live in Lima."

"Then that's where you're going?"

I explained my predicament.

"Look," he said laughing, "I'm no highway bum. I've got a good job, but with money still tight the way it is I try to save any way I can. So I've just hitchhiked into Chicago for a little vacation, and I'm on my way back to Marion. I've got money. Pull into the next gas station, and we'll gas up for the trip back to Lima."

I breathed a prayer of gratitude!

Many times while driving toward Chicago on Route 30 I have stopped at that gas station in Valparaiso just so I could roll down the window, draw in a deep breath, and say, "Fill 'er up!"

So far as I am concerned, experiences like this occurred far too often to be called coincidental. At my moment of need—whatever that need—God would intercede on my behalf. He is that kind of God—not some far-off celestial being but an intimate, personal, concerned friend. He knows the very number of the hairs on our heads. A sparrow cannot fall to the ground without His knowledge. He clothes the lilies, causes the grass to grow, but His greatest concern is to surround every one of His children with blessing and guidance.

Knowing God, walking with Him, depending upon His guidance became integral to my existence.

But I was only a novice in His ways.

I still am.

The successful Christian life consists of a triangle—reading the Bible, conversing with God through prayer, telling others of your faith. The first two dimensions had begun to mature in my experience. But the third, witnessing, had been largely neglected. True, I had not kept mute about my faith. I had witnessed. But my highest delight was in seeing God meet my temporal needs, get me out of problems, help me overcome obstacles in selling.

As a salesman, I felt guilty at times in using praise as a gimmick. I always tried to be pleasant with a client whether or not he gave me an order. Often I encountered profane men, a pathetic weakness, and my heart would be exercised by the desire to tell them of the transforming encounter they could have with Jesus Christ.

More often than not, however, I kept quiet. Telling a man he was a sinner, hellbent but for the grace of God, somehow didn't seem compatible with the career of a salesman.

I meant with all my grit and gumption to become a highly successful salesman.

On occasion, especially if business had been good, I would identify myself as a churchman. I loved my church, benefited much from its ministry, and made every effort to get back to Lima on Sundays so I could attend both morning and evening services.

But by no stroke of accuracy could you have called me an effective witness to the Christian faith.

It troubled me.

Through the years I have met many Christians. Whenever we get onto the subject of witness, these spiritual kinsmen of mine talk about how much they want to witness to their faith in Christ but how seldom and ineffectively they do it. One rarely runs across a Christian who is calloused on the matter. More likely one encounters those sweltering under the guilt of realizing how far they fall short of Christ's command.

This was my case.

I had an insatiable desire to succeed in business. Making money was the game of games, and I wanted to be home run king. I would fall asleep thinking of better ways to promote sales, dream about selling, and awaken the next morning with my head full of ideas on how to expand my market.

Though I remained very conscious of my faith and its significance to life, business came first. When I prayed, it was usually a prayer for God's blessing on my sales contacts.

In the desire to expand I began planning sales trips beyond my normal sphere of contact. It is typical of salesmen to think the grass will be greener on another street. One early foray took me out to Iowa, Nebraska, and South Dakota, where I determined to initiate a drove of new contacts.

I learned that a big country like America has a lot of different traits peculiar to each particular area. What had been good sales jargon in Ohio, Indiana, and Kentucky fell flat as I explored westward.

One night, blistered with discouragement, I pulled into a small town and checked into the hotel. Alone in my room I fell to my knees by the bed, my face burrowed into my hands.

"I've got troubles, Lord," I prayed. "I've been gone eight days, and I haven't even made expenses. People don't get the point of my presentation. It's so cold I have to pay to have my car pushed every morning. I need business. Please help me."

I knelt there in silence after that, waiting. I guess I expected God to reach down and touch me with love and assurance.

Instead I seemed to hear Him say, "Just a moment, Stanley. This is a two-way arrangement we have. You want me to bless you in your business contacts, and you know I've been doing it, but why should I help you any more? You don't do anything for me."

I didn't do anything for God?

Absurd!

Didn't I attend church every Sunday? Didn't I read my Bible faithfully? Didn't I pray about all my decisions, being careful to thank God for the many blessings He sent my way?

The more I thought about it, though, the more forcefully it hit me. My relationship to God had been pretty much of a one-way street. You could hardly call it doing Him a service to read the Bible, to attend church and thus receive inspiration for a richer life, to have the privilege of prayer whenever I needed divine assistance.

I took an honest look at myself that night and didn't like what I saw. I was pushing harder and harder in my business. I kept myself under pressure. I yearned for success. My relatives and friends were watching me. I wanted to impress them with my ability to emerge from shyness and ineptitude into a shining example of the local boy who makes good.

That hotel room became a sanctuary as I confessed to God my selfishness, my cowardice. "I want to give myself completely to You," I prayed. "From now on my whole life is Yours. Come in and take full control. Whatever You ask me to do, no matter what it is, I will submit to the best of my ability. I will look to You for the strength and guidance to do what You ask me to do."

I got to my feet and paced the floor. There was a newness in my heart, a buoyancy. God had led me to take a major step in my spiritual metamorphosis, the step of obedience.

Obedience!

It is my desire to make this one word central to my endeavor as a Christian. *Trust and obey,* the Bible tells us. It is a simple concept. It has profound overtones. And the very first step in obedience is to subordinate ourselves to the wisdom and the will of God.

When we do this, God will begin to ask for actions which denote obedience. These may seem fearful at times. Invariably, for this is the way God brings us to utter dependence, He will ask us to do things which are contrary to our own desires and preconceived notions.

In my case the command was to witness!

"How, God?" I prayed. "You know my mouth is a machine gun when it comes to talking about a product, but my tongue turns to stone when I think of warning men about their lostness, telling them of the redemption they can find in Christ."

I thought perhaps God was only testing me as He tested Abraham in the near sacrifice of Isaac. God knew my weakness. He surely didn't want me to discredit Him by poor witness.

Well, God doesn't ask for performance beyond our ability unless He provides the measure of strength necessary to project ourselves beyond ourselves. He did realize my fraility, my timidity. But in my Bible I had a couple of tracts I had received from our church. They were beautifully printed in contrast to many of the smudgy Christian leaflets I had seen in the past which, though I'm sure they were produced with every good intention, hardly did credit to the resplendent realities I was finding in the life with Christ.

These well-prepared leaflets impressed me. That's why I had slipped a couple of them into my Bible.

Here was a way I could witness. I could secure well-written, artistically produced Gospel tracts and give them to the people I met in my travels. Thus began a mode of witness which I still practice. Oh, I realize how many people look askance at the Gospel tract. But if we print literature to advertise worthwhile products, why isn't it just as feasible to use a similar method to promote the free gift of salvation provided in Jesus Christ?

And whatever our attitude may be, the fact remains that, as Jesus stood on the Mount of Olives prior to His ascension into heaven, the last words He said to His disciples were *"You shall be witnesses unto me."*

He has not rescinded the command, and the Christian only avoids it through disobedience.

30

5

I mentioned earlier how my great-grandfather took part in the gold rush of 1849. By no manipulation of genetics would I attempt to indicate that this laid the basis for my becoming a silver prospector. In fact, had the elder MacBeth known the manner in which his progeny would engage in the search for silver, he might have disclaimed relationship.

By this do not surmise that I stooped to some sort of chicanery in building my life in the business world. Everything I do is legitimate by every test or I wouldn't be doing it, but I do confess that the mode of my prospecting has unmistakable elements of the offbeat.

Being a child of the Depression had a lot to do with it.

I saw my parents agonize over the merciless financial famine which swept the country. Years of hard work to build up equity in their farm melted away—it was like watching strength drain from the dying form of a strong man—and something inside me formed a barrier against the idea of becoming involved in real estate or the expensive outlay of inventory. I wanted to buy low and sell high. I wanted quick turnover at a high profit. It was in my blood.

This gave impetus to the forming of the previously mentioned and short-lived Tam-o-shanter firm in which I collected waste oil from service station drainage pits and attempted to refine it. This was why I took to collecting out-dated photograph negatives and selling them to the firm in Valparaiso.

And this is how I got into the silver reclamation business.

I continued watching the magazines for get-rich-quick offers, looking for bits of information on possible ideas for exploitation. Then in 1932 I ran across a human interest item that ignited my imagination and convinced me I had at last found the signpost pointing out my destiny.

According to this news bit, the Eastman Kodak Company used some sixteen tons of silver each week in the manufacture of photographic film emulsion, eighty percent of which was washed off by the time an exposed negative reached the fixing bath.

It seemed incredible—nearly thirteen tons of silver going down the drain every week!

But that wasn't all.

A Cleveland inventor had developed a gadget capable of reclaiming this solvent silver but apparently had not been successful in convincing photo labs to cooperate in his venture.

It was a natural. Thousands of potential dollars in silver awaiting reclamation. An inventor with the answer but unable to sell his idea. Me, Stanley Tam, destined for mastery in the art of selling, eager to find a bonanza-type product.

But I was only a teen-ager when I clipped the article and knew I did not then possess the business initiative to undertake a venture of such magnitude. I put the information away with some other clippings, but I never forgot it. Again and again, browsing, I would reread it.

Then in 1936 when I had attained the confident age of twenty, I decided to look into the matter. So I scheduled a trip to Cleveland.

"Mr. Aukerman," I greeted the inventor, "I've come to help you get your silver collector into every photo lab in the country!"

"Well, young man!" he returned. "Come in! Come in!"

I added, "My offer, of course, depends on whether or not the device will do the trick."

"Oh, it works!"

"Can you demonstrate it for me?"

"You don't need to have the slightest qualms," he insisted. "I spent many years perfecting my invention. I faced every possible obstacle and made sure my device surmounted each potential problem. My collector is the answer to one of the greatest needs in American industry today."

He seemed a little too enthusiastic, and I grew skeptical.

"How does your invention work?" I asked.

He brought out an old box which looked as though it had been opened and closed many times, but not of late, and from it lifted his prototype.

"It's not very large," I said.

"I made it that way," he told me. "Too big and photo houses couldn't use it."

"Is it in use now?"

"Well . . ."

"When did you develop the invention?"

"A good while back."

"When?"

"1918."

My heart sank. There must be a snag. But then I looked at Mr. Aukerman. He seemed the honest type. Maybe he did have a valid money-making idea but just hadn't been able to market it. I breathed a prayer of thanks to God for letting me find this man, and a sense of peace came to my heart.

"You see inside here," Mr. Aukerman said tilting the unit toward me. "That's a battery in there. See those positive and negative plates?"

"I see."

"When the unit is placed in the fixing solution, the plates are activated, and the electricity generated draws the silver onto the plates. You collect these units from dealers, replace them with new units, and then take the silver to your headquarters and smelt it off."

"How much silver will a unit collect before it has to be smelted down?"

"Upwards to twenty dollars worth, I'd judge," the inventor told me. "Say seventeen or eighteen if the unit's working right."

"And how long should it take to collect that much silver?"

"Well, of course, that depends on how busy the photo lab is, how many negatives they wash and how often, but I'd say a unit would be ready for replacement every three to six months."

"One more question, Mr. Aukerman. What's it going to cost to make these units?"

"They're simple, as you see. I'd judge an enterprising young fellow like you could mass produce them for three or four dollars, maybe less."

33

My head began humming like an IBM machine.

Sixteen tons of silver used every week, eighty percent of it washed out into the sewers. A hundred units to begin with, even if they cost five dollars each and returned fifteen, would bring in a gross revenue above unit cost of ten to twelve thousand dollars.

A thousand units would gross over one hundred thousand dollars, and a photo lab would need two units per year as a minimum.

I could be a rich man! Within the year!

"You've patented this invention?" I asked cautiously.

"Naturally."

"The patent's for sale?"

"Not for sale, Mr. Tam, but I'll work out a contract with you on a royalty basis. Oh, I'm realistic. I know it's going to take a lot of work getting these into the hands of photo finishers. I'll not be exorbitant."

"Besides," I reminded him, "it's been over fifteen years since you developed this contraption."

We drew up an agreement, the terms somewhat better than I had hoped to maneuver.

Thus at the age of twenty-one Stanley Tam envisioned himself on the road to rousing success!

What I didn't realize was that, for the most part, photographers are the artistic type. They take pride in their work. They believe nothing to be more important than a photograph creatively composed, properly exposed, and expertly printed. They aren't particularly interested in sidelines, especially anything likely to detract from their artistic pursuits.

In my bounding enthusiasm I returned to Lima with the permission to manufacture Mr. Aukerman's silver collector. I quickly put together several of them. Then in eager confidence I set out to visit photo studios. But had I succumbed to my first inclinations I would probably still be selling household sundries.

"No, young man," was the typical reaction, "I don't believe I want to bother with your little toy here. I just don't think I want to mess with any extras."

"But it'll make money for both of us," I argued.

"You sure it won't pollute our chemicals?"

"How can it?"

"That's what we're asking you."

A few darkroom men decided to try the collector. But some didn't take care of the unit properly. Some lifted them out of the solution and forgot to put them back in. More than once the units themselves didn't function.

My anticipated bonanza threatened to become a catastrophic bubble.

I made the painful discovery in some instances that photo men let me into their plants because I had become the butt of their jokes.

"Hi-yo-silver!" they would yell out when I stepped inside the door. "How's it with you these days? How's your Indian friend, Tonto?"

Whereupon someone would whistle or ta-dum-te-dum the opening strains of the Lone Ranger's dramatic radio program.

"This here's the Lone Ranger?" a gum-chewing screech of a girl taunted one day. "He don't even wear a mask!"

I might have given up except for two reasons. First, I'm stubborn and don't give up easily. Second, in a growing number of labs the units performed exactly as expected. I was faced with the problem of properly educating photo men as to the use of the reclamation gadget and the problem of getting these men beyond the amusement and nuisance stage to the acceptance of my Tamco silver collector as a valid aid to their enterprise.

It was dogged work.

I made the simple units myself, spending a week or more in laborious manufacture, and then loaded them into the car and headed out for a week or two of selling. Not really selling. I placed the units at a small fee to the lab plus offering a royalty on all silver turned in.

There was one other slight problem.

Mr. Aukerman—and I don't for a moment hold it against him— hadn't told me he had entered into contracts with four previous individuals, each of whom had gone bankrupt!

But, I reasoned, these former individuals had probably lacked sales initiative. Plainly, the success or failure of the idea rested on sales. So I kept at it, determined to succeed.

Of course, I had virtually no financial backing. My father staked me to one hundred dollars to begin the venture; I had a car; and that was about it.

I tried to maintain optimism. I was establishing contacts with photo labs who would use my Tamco units, so in that sense I made progress. But distribution is always more costly than production, always more precarious, and when I could take time to evaluate costs and income it was invariably a sobering moment of truth.

Inevitably the day of reckoning came. Accounts payable crept slowly but unchecked to the point where I had to face facts. Income had also grown but too slowly to keep pace with the obligations inherent in a new enterprise.

I'll never forget that stifling moment. I had been pushing hard, building Tamco units, calling on photo labs from early in the morning until as late as anyone would listen at night. But I knew things were shaky.

To conserve on costs I had been working Ohio, down to Bellefontaine, Springfield, and Dayton, through Xenia and London to Columbus.

It was in Columbus where I looked my situation straight on. I had no funds for advertising in photo journals. I had only my own hands, my own lips to motivate my business. Goals set in the morning were never realized by night. I was whipped.

I decided to call it quits.

Numb with disappointment I packed my few belongings and headed home. I'd get a job or go back to selling. One thing was sure. I didn't ever again want any part of trying to set myself up in business.

"Why, God?" I prayed as I drove homeward. "Why?"

Then an incredible thing happened.

Just outside Columbus the Lord seemed to say to me, "Stanley, it doesn't need to be a disappointment. You don't have to go broke."

I was startled. The sense of God's voice seemed so unmistakable.

"You can see what's happened, God," I argued. "There just isn't enough going for me. Now if I had some capital . . ."

"You shouldn't be concerned about lack of finances. All you need is faith in Me, Stanley," the inner voice said.

"I do have faith, God."

"Enough to turn your business over to Me? To let Me run it for you?"

A hushed awe came over me. I was serious about my Christian life. I wanted God first in everything I did. But the concept of actually depending upon Him to run my business was as new as tomorrow's newspapers.

But wait a moment!

Had God spoken? Or was I so beaten down by my problems that I had the kind of frayed emotions which cause one to imagine things? Sure, I was disappointed about not making a go of Tamco. But maybe my pride had been hurt. Maybe all I wanted was to save face somehow. I really might be happier forgetting about building a business of my own.

"Remember the promise?" I again became conscious of the inner voice. *"My God shall supply all your needs according to His riches in glory by Christ Jesus."* The promise hasn't changed. You may claim it if you will. Turn your business over to Me. Let Me be responsible. Let Me supply the need. Don't you believe the provisions I have made for you in My Word?"

Such a sense of awe came over me that I slowed to a crawl on the highway. A truck snarled out of a curve and tailgated behind me, waiting for a spot of clear traffic. The driver honked angrily. I glanced up at him, wishing I could apologize, as he at last sped by me and cut in ahead.

"Lord," I prayed, slowly, deliberately, aloud, "could this really be? I want it if it's possible. I will turn my business over to You. Take it, God, and if You'll make it succeed, I'll honor You in every way I can. I promise!"

A wave of assurance bolstered my spirits.

Arriving home in Lima, I told my parents what had happened and asked my dad if he would consider helping me refinance the business.

He gave me twelve dollars. It was the best he could do.

But with that investment plus the twenty dollars I had in my pocket I went back to work. It was to be a long, hard pull, but I knew I would make it.

Through the years I have often used our silver collectors as an object lesson when addressing children and young people. Tamco collectors keep the silver from going down the drain, but when studios return the collectors to us in exchange for new ones the silver they send back is of no value due to its many impurities. We must put that silver into the refining fire where we submit it to 2300° of heat for two hours, bringing the impurities to the top so we can skim them off and thus produce a bar of pure silver.

Our lives are this way.

Salvation assures our relationship to God, but we still have impurities in our lives. Only the heat of testing can purge them out

37

and make us fit to serve our God. Often we complain when the fire gets hot. We should offer praise instead. For as Job wrote, *"He knows the way that I take. When He has tried me, I shall come forth as gold."*

I was to face many tests, some of them excruciating, but it was all in the divine plan, turning me again and again away from confidence in myself, firming my dependence upon the counsels of the Bible, undergirding my assurance in God's personal concern for me.

In fact, it is my opinion that suffering is a prerequisite to discovering the fullness of the life in Christ.

Did I say *suffering?*

In a sense, it is perhaps, but whatever the test, however deep and rugged the valley road, the vicissitudes God allows to shadow our upward way are always caused by the sunshine of His presence, the aura of which shall inevitably engulf us when the time of testing has subsided.

There is never a time when the Christian is without reason to sing the doxology!

6

You hear a lot of stories about traveling men.

Don't write off the lot of us as incorrigibles. Through the years my path has crossed with many who were solid citizens, faithful to their wives and families—like me, trying to make an honest living.

As I said previously, being a Christian qualifies you for membership in the world's finest fraternity. Traveling not only across North America but to other parts of the world as well, I have always found fellow Christians. It is like blood brothers meeting again after a long separation, for we have so much in common—our transformation through faith in the Son of God, our desire to serve and honor Him, our common hope for a rewarding eternity.

Of course, one of the best places to contact new Christian friends is in church, and whenever my itinerary held me out of town over a weekend, I always looked for a church where I could worship with fellow believers. Attending a worship service becomes increasingly vital when one realizes he is in a common act of spiritual fellowship with others of kindred faith.

Such a Sunday situation occurred during the summer of 1937 as a result of my first trip to Rockford, Illinois. Finding it such a pleasant city, I had no special desire to hurry home but decided instead to stay over the weekend and begin working my way back to Lima on the following Monday.

So on Sunday morning I set my alarm to avoid sleeping in, and after breakfast I headed out in search of a place to worship. I drove first one direction, then another, but for some reason didn't come upon a church that caught my interest. Then, turning off Seventh Street, my eyes picked out a large sign lettered *Christ Died for Our Sins.*

I decided the church displaying this sign was the place for me that morning.

A group of fellows met me outside, and one of them, an especially friendly chap, walked up and introduced himself.

"Hi, I'm Bob Miller."

"Stan Tam."

"You look like about the right age for our Sunday school class, Stan. Follow me."

In that instant I was among friends.

Tragedy had struck the church in the accidental death of one of the outstanding young people, and so there was an intense spirit of concern and involvement in both the Sunday school class and the worship service. I was impressed. My spiritual batteries got a good recharge.

"What are your plans for the afternoon?" Bob asked.

"Go back to the hotel," I said.

"Could I pick you up around three? Young people from various parts of the state are coming in for a memorial service. This fellow was our district youth society president. He was a great guy with a lot of good influence."

After the memorial service the emcee announced that out-of-town visitors would be guests of the local society for supper at a downtown restaurant.

"You're from out-of-town, Stan," Bob told me, "so you qualify."

"Aw, I don't want to leach any more of your hospitality," I said. "I'll just go back to the hotel."

"What do you mean, leach? You're already like one of the family."

"If I'm like one of the family, then you shouldn't be buying the groceries."

Bob slapped me across the shoulders. "We'll argue about that later. Come on!"

I had no more than sat down at my table when I sensed the wisdom of not having gone back to the hotel. Across from me sat the cutest blue-eyed girl I had ever seen. We got to talking and eventually introduced ourselves.

Her name was Juanita.

40

She had magnificent dimples and eyes that roamed across my face like sunbeams. I guess I conversed in circles because I was so taken up with just looking at her.

But then she said, "It's nice to have you to talk to. My boy friend was coming down from Minnesota, but at the last minute He couldn't make it."

My spirits sagged.

Oh well, it was a great scene while it lasted.

During those ensuing days, my thoughts often returned to the restaurant in Rockford. Because of my shyness and the paradoxical drive to make a success of Tamco, girls had not been high on my agenda. I looked forward to marriage but expected God to send the right one my way.

For several moments that Sunday afternoon this girl had seemed like the right one. But I determined to offer no contest. Besides, Rockford was too far away. I wasn't sure I could afford a courtship of that much geographical involvement.

A year later, however, in the spring of 1938, Juanita broke up with her Bunyan country boyfriend and, feeling a bit lonely, one evening, went to a friend's house to help put together some decorations for a youth retreat coming up at a nearby camp.

Then the doorbell rang.

It was Bob Miller from the church, asking Juanita and her friend to join some of his friends for the evening.

"We've got a fellow in from out-of-town for you, Juanita," Bob said.

"Who?" Juanita asked skeptically.

"A traveling salesman."

"Oh no you don't!"

"This guy's okay," Bob insisted. "He's a Christian."

"Is he from Rockford?"

"I told you—he's a traveling salesman. He was here the weekend of the memorial service for Hilding. I could see he sort of took a shine to you, though he never mentioned it."

Juanita was brimming with curiosity.

"This blind date is all my idea," Bob insisted. "The guy's out in the car and hasn't a clue you're the girl I picked out for him tonight."

"What's his name?"

"Stan."

"Stan who?"

"Tam."

"Stanley Tam?" Juanita mused, the name sounding vaguely familiar.

"You remember him. He sat across from you at the restaurant, when we—"

But Juanita was already on her way for her coat and hat.

Eight months later at the friendly church on Fourth Avenue and Sixth Street in Rockford, Illinois, she became Mrs. Stanley Tam.

She is a wonderful wife. You know, there just isn't any better basis for a marriage than two people who, in addition to being physically attracted to each other, have an avowed determination to put Christ first in their lives.

We've found it that way.

Through the years of our marriage my wife has been a perpetual sweetheart to me. I'm by nature a bit on the serious side, but I like a good joke and have been known to laugh till the tears rolled down my cheeks. Juanita can be delightfully funny, and many a night the recounting of her day's antics has taken the pressure off a rugged time at the office.

But she's also vitally alive spiritually. Her prayers have carried me through a lot of rough waters. Many times her perception has superseded mine in important decisions. I've had to be gone so much that years have literally been taken off our marriage. Juanita has yet to complain.

"You've got something to tell people, Stan," she says. "I like to feel I'm part of it, staying here at home with the children, praying for you."

I often speak to young people, and to the fellows I say, "It's okay to look for the blue eyes and dimples, but look even harder for a girl who puts Christ at the center of her life. Above all, seek God's will in your search for a mate. As my wife puts it, the best computer on earth couldn't have done any better than the way the Lord brought us together."

Rockford is a booming city with magnificent residential sections and huge industrial complexes, and Juanita could have married into more initial comfort than I was able to give her. For us, home was a house trailer, so we could be together as economically as possible.

She turned our house trailer into a small castle. I could face a rugged day on the road knowing she would be waiting for me, the trailer given a new (and always inexpensive) touch of her home-making skills or some special delicacy ready to pop out of the oven the moment I walked in the door. It was better than a mansion on Park Avenue, because it was always with me.

We parked in scenic areas whenever possible, along a lake or river, within view of rolling hills, or timberlands. I knew that Juanita would want a house of her own someday, but she had accepted the mobile home for this stage of our marriage and made believe she wouldn't have it any other way. At night we went over the day's business together and made plans for future sales forays. Except for face-to-face meetings with our clients she knew the business every bit as well as I did. Excitedly we watched our little Tamco fledgling begin to sprout feathers and test its wings.

"This is the secret," I told her. "Keeping costs down the way we do, laying the foundation ourselves for future expansion in the business. I'm sure this is why those other firms weren't able to make a go of the silver collectors."

"Plus one other," my wife reminded. "This isn't an ordinary business, you know. You gave it to God. If it succeeds, it's because of His blessing."

"Don't ever let me forget that, sweetheart."

We worked hard, living as cheaply as we could. I had many dis-appointments, but every day we grew stronger as more and more photofinishers began successfully using Tamco.

One evening near year's end for the business, we were back in Lima preparing new collectors for another jaunt on the road.

"Looks like we'll gross twelve thousand dollars this year," I said. "That's not a lot for a business, but we're growing. I'm thinking of raising our salary to fourteen dollars a week."

We laughed at that. We had pinched pennies all year, funneling every available dollar into Tamco operations.

"I can forsee something else, too," I said. "A house here in Lima where we can settle down permanently."

Juanita put her arms around me happily. She would have been willing to live in the trailer another five years. What better motivation did I need for trying to find a house as soon as possible?

I pushed harder than ever.

The day came when I felt we could begin house hunting. Juanita protested, insisting we couldn't afford to think of it yet.

43

"Real estate is about the best equity a young couple can invest in," I said. "Besides, we could use a house as our initial base of operations."

We found a place beyond what we had initially dreamed of and yet within the financial boundaries I had set in my mind.

I took it as from God's hand.

After this, I concentrated on areas adjacent to Lima so I could be home most evenings, not only to be near my wife but also because we worked so closely in the business.

The first of our four daughters was born, and now home became more meaningful to us than ever. Life was good and full. I wondered then as I do now how any man can settle for less than establishing a hearthside where God is genuinely at the center.

"Let's keep it this way," Juanita said. "So many people in business let prosperity rob them of their trust in God. That must never happen to us."

I admit I had moments when I feared this might happen, making me all the more determined to build a business as well as a home with God in the place of priority.

I little realized how literally God would take me at my word on this!

The business grew. I worked hard. By trial and error I began to acquire those touches of sales and management which build rapport and volume—facing situations which impelled me to believe God was on our side. I sensed a profound timing in everything. It awed me many times and consistently turned my thoughts to the realization of how much my success depended upon divine guidance and blessing.

This sense of awe, of realization, began to nag at my conscience.

One evening as we sat alone in our living room, Juanita noticed I had become especially quiet and inquired as to the reason.

"I've told you about the day on the highway just outside Columbus," I began, "when I told God that if He would take over the business I'd honor Him in every way I could."

Juanita nodded.

"God has been speaking to me about that promise, sweetheart."

"In what way?"

I studied my hands a moment. It was difficult to talk.

"That was a covenant I made with God," I said at last, "and a covenant with God is something a man had better keep."

"I agree," my wife said.

I was quiet for several moments.

"We surely do try to honor God in all we do," my wife said.

I continued to be quiet.

"Don't we?" she asked.

"We'd better," was all I said.

At last I said, "My problem is in being sure just how a man really involves God in business. It keeps hitting me, sweetheart, that I should be as concerned about God's place in our business as our pastor is for God's guidance in our church."

"I hadn't quite thought of it that way," Juanita said.

"Shouldn't it be? If a Christian doesn't identify God with everything he does, then something is wrong."

"Well," Juanita said, "ask God to show you if there's any more definite way the business can glorify Him."

"That's what I've been doing," I told her, "and it scares me."

"Why should it? All we both want is God's will. Whenever He shows us something to do, let's do it."

"You really mean that?"

"I surely do!"

"I feel God would have us take a big step of faith and make Him our senior partner in the business."

"How would we do that, Stanley?"

"Set up our papers so fifty-one percent of the stock belongs to Him."

Now it was my wife who did not speak. She looked at me intently, studying my face.

"What do you think?" I asked.

"We would give God half the business?"

"That's right."

"Can that be done?"

"I'd need to see a lawyer, but first I wanted to talk to you about it."

Juanita was quiet again.

"You know what that means," I said. "It means fifty-one percent of the profits will be set aside to go into Christian work."

My wife looked up. Her blue eyes had never been more penetrating, more beautiful.

"Honey," I asked, "what do you say?"

"Stanley, whatever God asks you to do obey Him."

7

As I said initially, the world looks somewhat askance at any layman who becomes overt in his display of spiritual objectives.

It seems obvious some Christians delight in being called fanatics. They consider themselves a heavenly people—so much so that, as one pulpit wit once put it, they become of little earthly good. For myself—since the time of my conversion—I have believed faith should be compatible to life, rather than transcendent to it.

Let me reemphasize my conviction that God intends the Christian experience to be the full, rich, satisfying, believable life. No amount of wealth or accomplishment or prestige can possibly give to a man the inner satisfaction possessed by the blue-collar man who has linked his life to Jesus Christ in a transforming relationship.

Kings and presidents, artists and tycoons—all have an inner need which only Christ can satisfy. *I am come that you might have life,* Jesus said, *and that you might have it more abundantly.*

My daily thirst is for this abundant life.

To have it, however, one dare not make of himself some kind of otherworldly oddity. True, we must be intent upon our Master's business as well as our own, but God put the laws of sales psychology into this world not so Milwaukee could sell more beer but so you and I could attract men to the Savior!

You can understand, then, the trepidation I felt as I contemplated the transfer of our stock into a non-profit religious foundation.

I could hear people say, "Hi-yo, silver! This Tam guy has really crossed his wires. He's not only gone fanatic; he's gone crazy." I've got a lot of personal pride. I want people to think well of me, and I don't like the idea of walking down the street and having someone look at me and point a spinning finger at his head.

But what does the Bible say?

Lay not up for yourselves treasures on earth, where moth and rust doth corrupt and where thieves break through and steal; but lay up for yourselves treasures in heaven . . . for where your treasure is, there will your heart be also.

Did Jesus mean these words? Are they applicable to you and me? If so, ought we to obey them?

I believe the answer to all three questions is *yes!*

From the outset of our Tamco business I had been a tither. Juanita and I still tithe the personal salary received from our business. But as one steward once aptly put it, the question isn't how much money I give to God but how much of God's money I keep for myself. For He made us, gave us our talents, our health, the very raw materials with which we work. *The earth is the Lord's and the fullness thereof,* the Psalmist wrote, *the world and all they that dwell therein.*

What's more, the Apostle Paul tells us, *We are laborers together with God, created unto good works.*

But before I proceed further, let me once again caution you. I'm Stanley Tam. You are you. God has a plan for my life. He has a plan for yours. He is the same God, but we aren't the same individuals, and He deals with each of us personally, intricately, specifically. The obedience He asks of me and the obedience He asks of you will in each case be tailored to our specific needs and qualities and, more strategically, to His perfect will for each of our lives.

In my case I had an insatiable thirst to make money. I love it. I like to promote, to see the company grow. I study our yearly and interim reports like a hungry hawk, evaluating, discovering, making checks and counterchecks. I'm interested in investments, too, and have been fortunate in making a number of profitable selections.

God knew my inner hungers, and when I told Him I wanted to turn my life over to Him completely He took me at my word. He began to set into motion forces which would lead me step by step into the fulfillment of His plan for me.

Some may scoff at the prospect of God's selecting a man's prime weakness as the area in which he is to exhibit his foremost steward-ship, and I admit to some disturbing moments on this score. But it is in the triumph over weakness that the grace of God becomes most manifest. Your strength is made perfect in weakness, our Lord tells us. The divine artistry makes an ill-tempered person gracious, a talkative woman poised, a promiscuous man moral, a selfish individual generous. For we must never forget that God is in the people-changing business.

In my case God knew my yen for making money. Had he left me undisturbed in this area, I could have become a proud, materialistic, self-centered spiritual misfit. But somehow I had found the wisdom to tell God He could have full control of me. I meant it, and God took me at my word. Thus, in asking of me the sub-mission of the greatest drive in my life, the thirst for making money, He removed a blighting influence and replaced it with inner peace and satisfaction such as I could never have otherwise known.

This was what I really wanted—what every thinking person wants—inner peace and satisfaction.

But I had to be obedient to His guidance!

In my case it meant carefully disciplined stewardship. I have no doubt but that other men may be able to run their businesses in the usual manner and be just as committed to God in the way they use their money. With me, however, it was a matter of nailing down the commitment.

Thus the day came when we walked into a lawyer's office and outlined our plan.

He listened dumbfounded.

When I finished he said, "Young man, you have a commendable attitude, to want to give the church half your money. But you and your wife are young. You need to plan for some security."

"I realize that, sir," I said.

"Now I'm not a financial counselor. Perhaps you've talked with a banker about this. You do realize, of course, how small your business is, even struggling. Who knows, you may never have much in the way of profits to think about."

"I expect the business to grow."

"I'm sure you do. But frankly, as an attorney I can't be party to this type of thing. Why don't you think it over for a while, say three months, and then come back and talk to me?"

"Then you won't draw up papers for me?"

"I can't, Mr. Tam. Not now. I'm sorry."

"What is the charge for your counsel?"

"No charge."

I thanked him and left.

"What are you going to do?" my wife asked.

"See another attorney," I told her.

As soon as possible I made the second appointment, trying this time to be more diplomatic with my presentation.

"My request is going to be a bit out of the usual," I began.

"I get a lot of unusual cases," the lawyer said pleasantly.

My spirits lifted.

"Well, sir, the situation is this. I'm in business. It's a small business. But it's growing, and I have every reason to believe it will one day be quite large."

"That doesn't sound like much of a problem," the lawyer said, smiling warmly.

"You see," I continued, "I'm a Christian. My faith is very vital to me. What I have is a direct result of God's special intervention on my behalf. So what happens in the future also depends directly upon His blessing. What I'd like to do, the real reason I'm here, is that I'd like to make God my senior partner."

He looked aghast.

My spirits ebbed.

"I'd like you to make out a legal paper," I continued, "whatever's necessary, to the effect that my wife and I are turning over fifty-one percent of our business to the Lord."

"Well, young man," he said pensively after a lagging silence, "you have a wonderful attitude, to want to give the church half your money."

It was as though he had a recorder in his throat playing back the first attorney's sentiments.

"I've heard this before," I complained impatiently. "You're the second lawyer I've consulted."

"The first attorney refused to draw up the paper you requested?"

"That's right."

"Well, I'm afraid this one must render the same decision."

"But I'm rational," I argued. "This is something my wife and I have thought through carefully. We've asked God for guidance and are sure of His direction. Haven't we a right then to take whatever legal steps we find necessary?"

He looked at me, not speaking.

"I don't want to seem abrasive," I continued, "but I've got to have a paper drawn up, so I guess all I can do is sit here until you agree to do it."

He smiled wanly. "You're serious about this, aren't you?" he said.

"Dead serious."

He pondered a moment.

"Please help me," I pleaded.

"Well," he said slowly, "I suppose the problem is that men like me are in business not because people want to serve God the way you seem to do but because so many people are prone to break God's laws."

"You'll help me?" I prodded.

He was quiet another moment.

Then he said, "I tell you what I will do. Even this is against my better judgment, but I'll make out your will. I'll put your wishes into your will."

"But I'm young. I could live another sixty years!"

He chuckled. "That wouldn't exactly be a catastrophe, now would it?" Growing serious he added, "Shall I draw up the will? That's the best I can do for now."

With considerable hesitation I agreed to his suggestion.

"I just don't understand it," I told my wife that night.

We sat at the table about to spend a few moments in Bible reading and prayer as has been our custom since marriage.

"What's so abnormal about me? I'm a human being. I love you as intensely as any man can love his wife. I like good food, a comfortable house, decent clothes, a good car. So why can't it be just as normal to want God to have the key spot in our business?"

"Don't be discouraged."

"I'm trying not to be."

"You did the best you could. God knows that. Maybe what happened today was the first step He intended you to take."

"We've got to obey God, sweetheart."

"Did we disobey Him today?"

"No, but—"

"Then let today stand for itself."

"I love you." I whispered and reached for her hand.

"We live in a mixed-up world, Stanley. It's a dark world with a

50

lot of confused, frightened people in it. But we're different. Not because of who we are or anything we've done but because of our relationship to God."

"Keep talking. I need it."

"God has a plan for our lives, for yours especially. I'm so sure of it. Don't doubt. Let Him lead you an event at a time. Let Him make you an example worthy of the scrutiny of others, of people who are looking so desperately for answers these days. Maybe our lives can give out a little light to help some of these poor folks discover what we've found."

"I love you," I whispered again.

"Read."

I opened the Bible.

We had just begun reading in Proverbs, the book that has given me a lot of counsel through the years.

Trust in the Lord with all your heart, and lean not unto your own understanding. In all your ways acknowledge Him, and He shall direct your path.

It was good to know!

8

The time came when I questioned the wisdom of settling down in the house in Lima.

Since Tamco was pretty much a one-man band—building the collectors myself and then hitting the road and placing them—I faced obvious limitations. There are only so many hours in the day, and a salesman can't barge into an establishment and expect priority time. Not only did I need to look for new business if we were to keep growing, but the only procedure I saw as workable was to place the silver collectors with photo studios personally, pick them up and replace them with new units when sufficient silver had been collected for smelting.

It was a laborious procedure, and we dreamed of the day we could have representatives out doing this for us. The hitch, of course, was that with postwar salaries beginning to spiral, we were a long stretch away from being able to afford the cost of putting men on the field.

Then one day in Mankato, Minnesota, when my wife was with me on a trip, she picked up a paper and discovered the disturbing news of a drop of nearly three cents per ounce in the price of silver. The next day the price dropped two more cents, and thereafter a cent a day until it finally levelled at thirty-five cents.

I was terrified.

We had several bars at home waiting to be sold, and our loss was somewhere around five hundred dollars.

We drove to Minneapolis to check with a refiner there but could get no satisfaction, so we headed home, both of us very discouraged.

As we drove toward Lima I said, "I don't see how we can operate on thirty-five cents an ounce. I can't stay on the road because there isn't enough money in it."

I hadn't been so discouraged in years.

"Could we handle our business by mail?" Juanita asked.

"I doubt it. The photographers always save their collectors until I come around asking for them. They want as little bother as possible."

"We could try mailing them out and having the photographers mail them back."

"Oh, I'm game to try," I said, "but I'd better look for something else to do to supplement our income. Like maybe house trailers. I know enough about house trailers to start selling right away."

"Let's not jump to conclusions," Juanita counseled, "until we see what happens."

Shortly before this we had established headquarters in a basement, hiring a young fellow to run it for us while we were out on the road. I had to tell him we didn't need him any longer.

We tightened our belts every way we could.

"Don't go out looking for another job right away," Juanita said. "First, let's try direct mail and see what happens."

We began sending out reminders through the mail. I was highly skeptical, but to my amazement the silver collectors began to come in, and we would mail out new units to replace them. We also tried promoting sales by direct mail with heartening results.

Now at last our volume began to grow. And I never did get around to looking for a supplementary job.

This kind of thing has happened so often in our business. I like to think I have reasonable intelligence, and I try to apply that intelligence to the functions of our business, but many times it is a circumstance rather than my ingenuity which leads us into a whole new surge of growth and opportunity. This is another reason why I'm so convinced that God orders our ways for us when we turn our affairs over to Him.

It wasn't long until I was able to go back to the attorney and convince him we should literally make God our senior partner. Thus came into being the Stanita Foundation, which I will tell you about in more detail later.

In any business growth gestates problems.

I became increasingly dissatisfied with our silver collector. It had a few bugs in it, and we began receiving a disturbing number of letters from photographers reporting difficulties. Actually, if the customer would have carefully followed the instruction sheet sent with each collector, he should have had no difficulty. But photographers are busy men. So the solution was somehow to come up with a more foolproof collector.

By Christmas of 1943 the situation had deteriorated to a disturbing degree.

We went to Rockford for the holidays. One night I felt a compelling need to place this problem in God's hands. There was gaity in the house, and I tried to be a good sport and enter in, but when the others had retired, I told Juanita I needed some time to be alone.

She left me and went to bed.

Kneeling by the couch I began to pray. I didn't know what to do.

"Lord," I prayed, "I'm going to stay here on my knees until You give me the answer. I'm licked, just as I've been in the past, and I don't know which way to turn. Please help me."

On and on I prayed into the morning hours, but there seemed to be no answer. My heart grew increasingly heavier.

Then, almost audibly, the words came to me: *No good thing will He withhold from them that walk uprightly.*

I stumbled to my feet.

"Lord, thank you!" I exclaimed.

Then I got to thinking. Was that a quotation from the Bible? I didn't remember hearing it before. My mother-in-law's Bible was nearby. I picked it up. It had a concordance, and in a few moments I turned to the Eighty-fourth Psalm to read: *The Lord God is a sun and shield: the Lord will give grace and glory. No good thing will He withhold from them that walk uprightly.*

It was at this time Mr. Aukerman, the man in Cleveland from whom I had secured the first unit, developed a greatly improved silver collector. As soon as I heard about it, I got in touch with him. We drew up a contract allowing me the right to manufacture the new collector. The contract specified that I was to pay him royalties, that I was not to question his patent, and that if I ever quit using collectors, I was to turn my records over to him so he could service the customers.

54

Mr. Aukerman and I had excellent relationships until 1945 when I discovered that a man in New Jersey was manufacturing and distributing collectors identical to our own.

I wrote to Mr. Aukerman and asked if he wished to initiate legal proceedings against the infringer. His reply puzzled me. He wrote: "Mr. Tam, you have exclusive rights to my patent. If you want to stop this man, that is your privilege."

So I notified the New Jersey firm, gave them our patent information, and instructed them to desist from any further activity.

Their attorney informed me they had made a careful search and discovered that Mr. Aukerman's patent was faulty. The new silver collector was public domain. I began to wonder if this was why the inventor refused to press litigation himself. Other thoughts came to my mind. Why pay two hundred dollars per month royalty on a no-good patent?

I consulted a patent attorney in Dayton. He agreed to research the matter for me and two weeks later wrote: "The New Jersey attorney is correct. Mr. Aukerman's patent is faulty, and he cannot defend it in court. My advice is that you pay no more royalties."

"But," I wrote back, "what about the contract I signed with Mr. Aukerman?"

Replied the patent attorney, "Since the patent is invalid, he cannot hold you to the contract. If you wish, we will take over the case and legally notify the inventor that he cannot hold you to the contract."

It bothered me, but I gave my consent.

Mr. Aukerman was furious. He sent his attorney to see me.

"We think you should continue paying the royalties," the attorney said.

"But the patent is faulty," I argued.

"Do it as a matter of good faith," he urged.

"I'm sorry," I said. "I'll not do it. If the patent were valid, I wouldn't hesitate for a moment. But the patent is no good. You know it wouldn't hold up in court. I'll stand on my rights as a citizen."

That ended the matter.

Or so I thought.

Three years passed. Business continued to boom. Then an evangelistic crusade was planned for our city, and I accepted the responsibility of spearheading prayer groups.

I went from church to church on the night of the midweek meeting, and pastors often turned the entire service over to me, permitting me to speak about the coming crusade and to urge all in attendance to get behind the effort with their prayers and their support.

One night, speaking to a group, I said, "Lima, like so many cities in America, needs a real touch from God. In the past the church has seen what happens when genuine revival touches a community. Let's believe such an awakening can come to our area.

"But you know," I continued, "we don't need to wait until the campaign for revival begins. We could ask God for such a manifestation of His Spirit right now."

A moving sense of spiritual oneness came to us, as men and women implored God to give them a fresh encounter with the Holy Spirit.

And then God began speaking to me!

"Stanley, how can you pray for revival when all is not right in your own life? Look at the way you have treated that inventor."

"Lord," I prayed silently, "we're not praying for Mr. Aukerman tonight. We're praying for our city-wide evangelistic crusade."

But the voice of God was persistent. "You signed a contract with Mr. Aukerman. You agreed to pay him royalty, and you agreed not to question the patent. Do you know you perpetrated falsehood when you went to the attorney and questioned the patent?"

"But maybe that's why he put the clause in the contract," I argued. "He knew the patent was faulty. Can't I stand on my rights as a citizen?"

"There are two kinds of laws, Stanley. There is man's law, and there is My law. You could drink a quart of whiskey tonight and not break any law in the state of Ohio, but you would break My law. By whose standard are you living, man's or Mine?"

I was like Jacob wrestling with God. The prayer meeting continued in a spirit of joyous and searching renewal, but I withdrew to the arid silence of my heart.

I didn't tell anyone about my experience, not that night or all the next day. But on the second day, a Saturday, I had a luncheon appointment with a friend and, being so miserable, decided to ask his advice.

His name was Steve. He was a real friend.

Steve could have shrugged his shoulders and said, "Forget it,

Stan. You give God some of your money. You're active in church work." But he didn't.

The Bible says, *Blessed are the wounds of a friend*. Steve looked me squarely in the eye and said, "If what you tell me is true, Satan has an accusation against you at God's throne. You'll never have any spiritual power in your life until you obey the Lord in this matter."

I made immediate plans to contact Mr. Aukerman, finding that he now lived with his daughter in Wilmington, Delaware.

"The prodigal son wants to come home," I wrote to the old inventor. "If you will be in Wilmington, Delaware, a week from Thursday, use the money I am enclosing to send me a telegram, and I'll make arrangements to come."

He sent a telegram confirming the date.

After the prayer service at our church the following week, my wife drove me to the train station.

"I'm proud of you," she whispered.

"It's this business of obedience, honey," I said. "I've got to learn to obey God in everything."

There were tears in her eyes as we kissed goodbye, but she was also smiling.

Mr. Aukerman's daughter met me at the train. I thought we would drive to her home. Instead she took me to the skyscraper office building of the Dupont company, which has its headquarters in Wilmington. I didn't ask any questions as we ascended the elevator, but I was intensely curious.

We got out at the sixth floor, and she led the way down the hall to a suite of offices.

It was the office of a corporation attorney!

I felt like Daniel walking into the lion's den as we stepped inside where an attorney, a Mr. Carlson, waited to see me.

"I work for Mr. Carlson," Aukerman's daughter explained. "My father thoughts perhaps you wouldn't mind explaining to him what you have in mind."

I began to feel less apprehensive.

"Your letter is rather brief," Mr. Carlson said, "but we think we understand your intentions. Could you give us more details?"

I try never to preach to people but rather to share my experience as a Christian. But the strong compulsion came to me this day that I should tell my story, my whole story, to these people.

57

They listened intently as I paced the floor—relating my past, telling of the farmer's wife who pointed me to Christ, of my early business discouragements, of the way God had clearly spoken to me about the matter of the royalties and how I, rebellious, tried not to heed.

"I'm here today," I said, "because I have sinned against Mr. Aukerman, and I want to make restitution."

The attorney and Aukerman's daughter looked at each other in mute amazement.

We spent several hours negotiating an agreement. It was an enriching experience, no rancor, only the desire to do what was right. On several occasions I was asked to leave the room while they discussed points between themselves.

Then the attorney named a sum of money and said, "If you would be willing to pay this amount, Mr. Aukerman will be happy to give you a signed statement that you have full right to his silver collector with no further royalties due him."

The amount was within five hundred dollars of what I had felt would be a fair settlement!

An enormous load rolled off my heart as we signed that agreement. Not only had things been put right between myself and Mr. Aukerman, but also the clogged channels were cleared between myself and my Lord.

In December of that year Mr. Aukerman suffered a sudden cerebral hemorrhage, was unconscious for two weeks, and died a few days after Christmas. When I received the letter telling of his death, I buried my face in my hands.

"Dear God," I prayed, "what if I had delayed obeying You? He could have one day stood before Your judgment throne and accused a hypocrite of standing in his way."

Two weeks after the funeral the inventor's daughter sent me one of the most treasured letters I have ever received. "He forgave you fully," she wrote. "He had his picture taken just after you were here and asked me to send one to you. But then he took suddenly ill, and I didn't get it attended to. It is enclosed."

It was my subsequent privilege to be a guest in this woman's Wilmington home. She now has a personal and vital faith in Christ.

Do you wonder why?

9

After that first year when we so successfully tested the use of the mails as a substitute to barnstorming the Midwest, our business grew, slowly at first like a rocket after countdown, then with surging momentum. We did sixteen thousand gross the second year, then forty-five thousand, then ninety thousand, one hundred and fifty thousand, multiplying year after year.

But God continued to discipline us.

We had been selling reclaimed silver to a firm in Chicago, but as our volume grew it occurred to me that we might be wise to have more than one outlet for marketing our bullion.

So we sent a shipment to a refiner in the East who promptly wrote back stating we had neglected to enclose our Internal Revenue stamps, whereupon I wrote that I was in the dark as to what they were talking about.

The refinery sent me a copy of Government Regulation No. 84 with a curt note suggesting I read it if I had in mind staying in the silver business. The bulletin stated that anyone not having a license was classified as a speculator and obligated to pay fifty percent tax.

I was horrified.

My first temptation was to stick with the first refinery who had asked no questions, probably supposing we were taking care of the tax from our end. But as a Christian and as a good citizen, I knew I had to face up to my error.

I called the local IRS office, who referred me to the Miscellaneous

Tax Division in Toledo. There the man in charge got out the book of regulations. "That's right," he said. "You must have a license to operate a silver refinery, but I don't know what to do with a company like yours where you have already operated for ten years without one. I'll write up your case and send it to Washington for them to decide."

Washington sent back a report indicating I owed twenty-three thousand dollars in delinquent taxes!

The news hit me like a head-on collision, and that night after the family had retired, I slipped into the living room and got down on my knees to cry out to God once more. I was full of complaints. I told Him how tough it was to run a business, how much easier it would be to get an eight-hour job and leave all the pressure to somebody else; and the Lord in His wisdom let me get my martyr complex thoroughly aired.

Then, as He had so often spoken before, He said to me, "Stanley, haven't I answered prayer for you in the past? I know this is a large request, but I am an omnipotent God. I can answer prayer for big problems as well as little ones."

I confessed the sin of unbelief and in childlike faith cast my burden onto the Lord.

I've had people say, "That's good psychology, Mr. Tam, but it doesn't pay the bills."

Such people have forgotten something. Vital faith and mere religious observances can be as different as noon is from midnight. God is not some concept we formulate in our thinking. *Know ye that the Lord He is God,* the Bible assures us. *It is He that has made us, not we ourselves. We are His children and the sheep of His pasture.*

God is not a liar. He will do what He says He will do. Nor does He play cat-and-mouse with His children. He designed us to become the recipients of His mercy, His grace, and His love. What folly, what sheer nonsense, to say God is dead, a mere figment of the superstitious past.

God is alive!

As my senior partner, He made a special trip to Washington, D. C., to plead our case. He knew whom to see, what heart to touch. I didn't have costly legal fees. No volumes of papers to file. No unnerving red tape.

The Miscellaneous Tax Division in Toledo received word from

Washington as follows: "If it is equitable with your office, we would like to forgive Mr. Stanley Tam of Lima, Ohio, for all the tax with the exception of four hundred and sixty-seven dollars."

But while God does honor us when we make our business His business, we have the clear injunction of Scripture that we are to *be not slothful in business.* A man can't take a haphazard attitude toward his work, carelessly spend money, and then expect God to pick up the loose ends and bring him out on top. I've talked to men who were in real financial difficulty. They heard me give my witness and then came to me expecting me to give them some kind of key to the treasury of heaven.

Like any businessman, I've had to learn by trial and error. Sometimes there was a lot of error involved.

Now I know the Bible assures us that God shall supply all our needs. Some Christians think this means you can make yourself comfortable while God does all the worrying, but I don't believe it. I met a fellow once who made a practice of deliberately going into debt so his faith would be stimulated to trust God to supply his needs. That fellow went bankrupt!

No, God has equipped us to think for ourselves, to make decisions, to exert initiative. You can't expect God to do your thinking for you. What you can do is yield your mind, your body, your strength to Him and ask Him to guide your thoughts and your actions. God did not create you as a puppet but as an intelligent, resourceful human being.

At the outset of my business career I began setting standards and goals which served to discipline my conduct and objectives.

In over thirty years as a businessman, for example, I've borrowed money only one time. That was twenty-five thousand dollars on a one-year note at the bank for the purchase of our first building. Otherwise, we operate on company-initiated capital. When I've needed money I've asked my senior partner for it, and He's given it to me. Now I know business today is operated on borrowed money, and I'm not opposed to people borrowing, but so far as I'm concerned, I'd always rather collect the interest than pay it.

Let me comment a moment on what I mean by asking my Senior Partner to supply needed capital.

I like to read the biographies of successful men, particularly Christians, and few life stories have affected me so profoundly as that of George Mueller, the English orphanage man whose prayers of faith resulted in millions of dollars being contributed to Christian work in Britain. This money came because Christian people sensed the need in those days to exercise obedient stewardship as a result of Mr. Mueller's intercession.

But contributions are only one form of stewardship. The way a man conducts his business and the way a woman watches the household budget are both potential acts of good stewardship.

So, when I have needed money in our business I haven't asked God to send down some kind of green manna from the skies. I haven't expected a well-heeled Christian businessman to give me a handout. On the contrary, I've asked God to show me how I could upgrade the effectiveness of our business operations so we could generate the needed capital. In other words, I have asked Him to illuminate my mind and guide our business decisions, and He has wonderfully answered this kind of prayer thousands of times.

My theory is that God has given each of us a brain and expects us to use it. There are laws in business just as in anything else, and if we use our heads in harmony with those laws, we stand a good chance of success.

But, though I believe in application of good principles in business, I place far more confidence in the conviction that I have a call from God. I'm convinced that His purpose for me is in the business world.

My business is my pulpit.

Perhaps you suspect, then, that what has happened to me is coincidence, that a strictly secular individual might have experienced some of the same crises I have faced and come out on top as well.

Let me speak to that point.

I frankly don't believe I'm as good a businessman as our financial statements indicate. I believe I operate far above my natural capacity and simply am not the type who builds our kind of multimillion dollar annual volume with the fine profit margin we've been able to maintain—ten percent after taxes—which is exciting with business as it is today.

I consider myself something like the tail of a kite. As long as I'm attached to the kite I can't help but succeed. I must keep clean, obedient, and to do this I make it a point every day and often several times during the day of committing myself anew to the Lord.

I'll try to explain how this works.

62

The Bible abounds with God's invitation for us to involve **Him** in the details of our lives. The satanic deceit is for man to relegate God to organ preludes and stained-glass windows and profound liturgies—and all of these embellishments have their place—whereas God wants to be personal in our lives. We are not to think of Him flippantly as a "good guy" or even as "the man upstairs" but rather as One to be involved with our most intimate selves.

Throughout the day I quietly commit to the Lord whatever comes up in my activity. I ask Him for guidance when I have problems and thank Him for help when I work out answers to those problems. It isn't necessary to get on one's knees or to recite a specific prayer. All God asks is for our minds and our motives to be in assent to His will, acknowledging His power, and this can be a moment's thought, even an attitude of the heart.

I think the key to the whole situation is for us to realize that God depends on us to validate His existence and His ability to make something out of a man. This narrows down to one word—witness. Being a witness is more than getting up on a soapbox and quoting a few Bible verses. Being a witness means to let ourselves serve as billboards, as living exhibits, attesting the truth that God is alive and at work.

Think of the wonderful privilege of being a witness to the reality of God! What in all the world could make life more worth the living?

I know Satan would like to decimate my witness, to paint me into some kind of corner where in a few iniquitous moments my spiritual effectiveness would be ruined. I've known too many fine men who've fallen prey to the devil's wiles for me to face this kind of eventuality complacently.

In fact, it is my conviction that the closer we walk with God, the harder Satan tries to bring us down. Here again the Bible promises us we can be *more than conquerors* in Christ.

But we must keep our eyes on Him!

Let me just say something about our being able to make it in the silver business.

You'll recall my mentioning four other companies who had gone bankrupt—a fact unknown to me when I first approached Mr. Aukerman about manufacturing rights on the unit he had developed.

Could I have struck it lucky and made a success without God's help?

I doubt it.

As you can surmise, silver collecting gives all kinds of opportunity for dishonesty. When I stopped by photo shops and asked for the collectors I had placed there, these men didn't know how much money would be coming to them. I could have set my price. But I determined to give honest measure to the fraction of an ounce, and slowly but surely this fact began to sink in.

Many of these photographers had been cheated so badly in the past they didn't want anything to do with silver collectors. But by the application of strict Christian principles on our part, many of them regained confidence. There were photographers, however, a good many of them, who pointedly refused to have anything to do with me. Knowing some of the things that had happened in their past experience, I can't blame them.

I went into a large processing center in Michigan one time and asked for their business. They had been taken to the cleaners in the past and didn't even want to talk to me.

But then I saw a couple of the men whispering among themselves.

"Say," one of them spoke up, "are you the fellow who gives half of his profits to the church?"

"That's right."

"Then I guess we can trust you. Sure, you can put silver collectors in here."

This became one of our best accounts.

Always remember, though, that whereas God often offers to work *with* us, His usual pattern is to work *through* us. He inspires our minds, guides our hands, directs our feet. His promise is: *I will instruct you and teach you in the way you shall go. I will guide you with my eye.* He instructs us and guides us, but the doing and the going is left to us.

The requisite for this instruction and guidance is always to be clean and obedient. When you seek to follow the Christlike life, you can expect God to check up on you, to test your motivations.

Once, for example, we made a shipment of silver to a refiner in Chicago, expecting a check in the amount of two thousand dollars. Instead we received a check for five thousand dollars.

And believe me, it was at a time when we could have used an extra three grand!

Was I tempted to keep the money? Of course I was. But I had a commitment to God. Not just a partial commitment, not just when I was in a jam and needed help, but a commitment involving every transaction and every moment of every day.

I wrote a brief note to the Chicago firm suggesting they do a new assay. They, thinking I was displeased with the amount received, agreed and were amazed when they learned of the three thousand dollar error. I received a two-page letter of gratitude. By mistake, two assay numbers had become interchanged, and there was no way of tracing it without my letter.

A short time later on a trip to Chicago Mr. Goldsmith, vice-president of the firm, invited me to lunch with four other gentlemen.

"Mr. Tam," Goldsmith asked as we sat eating, "what do you mean when you say God is your senior partner?"

"It's a long story," I said.

"We'll take the time."

For the next hour it was my privilege to tell these men of the miracle God had wrought in my life—the redemption of my soul and the guidance for my activities.

I didn't detect the slightest skepticism in their eyes. When you refund a man three thousand dollars, he believes you when you tell him why you did it!

10

My life is far from a perpetual succession of crises.

Observers from the ranks of the uncommitted have often accused us Christians of morbidity. We sing about the burdens of life. We pray about our rheumatism, our arthritis, and our impending surgeries. Too often the sermon that moves us most is the one describing the valley rather than the mountaintop.

Surely God never intended the Christian adventure to be so characterized.

Nehemiah the prophet declared, *The joy of the Lord is your strength,* and Jesus said, *These things have I spoken unto you, that my joy might remain in you, and that your joy might be fill.* Now I realize that even though the test of our joy comes when inclement circumstances disrupt the normal trend of life, these are but occasionals. The day-by-day mood of the Christian should be one of genuine exuberance, a tone of voice and a hue of countenance that are not mere facade but erupt from the reservoir of spiritual maturity.

I also believe God can motivate us in moments of pleasure. I have spoken at summer youth encampments, and the very sight of clean, purposeful, Christian young people has gripped my heart and deepened my determination to help the youth of our land—and we have hosts of good kids in this country—to discover the positives of the life in Christ.

But God knows us so much better than we know ourselves. He

knows that given nothing but sunshine we would grow careless and only play when we have work to do. So He sends the clouds, the shadows, to draw us apart so He can speak to us more clearly. It may be a problem, a disappointment, an impending danger, or it may be God will burden our hearts in such a way that we know He has a special message for us and thus needs for us to seclude ourselves for prayer, Bible exploration, and meditation.

The latter was the case with me back in the fall of 1945. All was well in the business. We had set up the Stanita Foundation controlling fifty-one percent of our stock and had been able to dispense considerable funds to various aspects of Christian work. I was active in the work of our church, particularly the Sunday school, which showed a very encouraging growth.

I believe laymen should be active in the work of the church, and I am particularly sold on Sunday schools. In 1941 when our church named me superintendent of the Sunday school, we had an average enrollment of eighty-six. I had many big ideas, such as staging a contest with a church in Toledo, but in the first year our average attendance dwindled to eighty-two.

Attending the Winona Lake Bible Conference the following summer, I picked up two books. One was titled *How to Put Your Sunday School Across,* and the other was a book on spiritual revival by Charles Finney. The first book was excellent, but it was Finney's book that ignited a response in my heart—particularly the chapter on "Hindrances to Revival," in which I saw my pride, my self-dependence, my sin brought out as pointedly as though the book were a personal evaluation.

Renewal came to my life as I asked God to remove from my heart anything which might hinder my effectiveness as a Sunday school worker. Inevitably things began to change.

Previous Sunday school offerings had averaged five dollars per week and were used to buy coal for the church. I asked the board if we could spend the money on the children. We painted, cleaned the basement, purchased equipment, and began building room partitions as money permitted.

Attendance grew. The adults began to take notice. A gift of eight hundred dollars made possible the purchase of two buses.

Average attendance increased to one hundred and nineteen the next year, then one hundred and sixty-four—up again to over two hundred, and it kept growing.

It was wonderful to see. Yet my heart was heavy. The Lord seemed to be saying, "Stanley, you are doing well. But remember that trip you took out to Iowa and Nebraska? Remember the night in the hotel room when you told Me I could have every bit of you? This isn't really true, is it?"

I was a little bewildered.

A Sunday school convention would be coming up in Chicago soon, and I had thought of attending.

I said to my wife, "Why don't you slip home for a few days while I go to the convention in Chicago? I'll attend sessions during the day, but I want to spend the evenings alone in the hotel room. I've got to get something settled in my life."

"Anything special?"

"I'm not sure. I feel restless for some reason."

She touched my arm.

"I'll pray for you," she said.

Actually, I knew why God had so heavily burdened my heart, but I was trying to evade the issue. All through the summer I had been conscious of the fact that, whereas God had given me the talent for selling, I was using the talent for secular pursuits.

I attended the convention and tried to take a few notes during the sessions, but whenever I had a spare moment, I slipped up to the hotel room to read my Bible, pace the floor, and pray.

A number of Bible verses came to my attention, verses such as: *You shall be witnesses unto me . . . He that gathers in summer is a wise son, but he that sleeps in harvest is a son that causes shame. He that goes forth weeping, bearing precious seed, shall doubtless come again rejoicing, bearing his sheaves with him . . . He that wins souls is wise.*

"But Lord," I argued, "look how the Sunday school has grown. And people know my stand as a Christian. Isn't that a witness? You've prospered the business so we have money to give to Christian organizations that are active in soul-winning. Isn't that enough?"

"I want *you* to be a soul-winner, Stanley."

"I?"

"I've helped you overcome shyness and have given you the talent for selling merchandise. Now I want you to use this talent to persuade men of their need for salvation."

"But I give out tracts, Lord! I've distributed thousands of them!"

In my heart I didn't want to resist the divine compulsion. Actually, I was afraid. Sometimes, you know, the man who seems to be the most extroverted is really an introvert deep down inside. Thus I'm convinced God must have the credit for success in our business —if for no other reason than the way He has helped me overcome my natural reticence.

What frightened me most was the thought of telling men they were lost, sinners needing the atonement of the cross. I'm not the kind to "lay a man to filth," as they say in common parlance.

As the days of the convention neared conclusion, I could find no settled peace in my heart. Tacitly at least, I told God I would try to contact men personally, telling them of their need for salvation, though I didn't know how I would do it. What confused me most was that, though it was a fine convention, I found myself less and less able to concentrate on Sunday school matters. I was sold on Sunday school work (and still am), but a man has only so much time in each day, and I kept feeling this strong compulsion that my time was to be devoted otherwise.

I went for a walk through the Loop, along Madison, down LaSalle. I came to Randolph, the theater section. Huge marquees ablaze with light heralded the latest Hollywood releases, the biggest stars. I had developed a hatred for the movies. I'm sure there have been producers who wanted to say something worthwhile on the screen, but I'm much more sure Hollywood has played a strong contributing role in the moral and social problems we face today.

Yet, despite my aversions, those marquees reminded me of a strange compulsion I had had on several occasions during the summer—the idea of securing a motion picture projector and some Christian films and using them in home-to-home evangelism.

Whenever the thought occurred I tried to stifle it. In my prejudiced mind the motion picture was a tool of evil. I had even spoken out against the trend toward showing religious films in churches. To me the motion picture was a tool of Satan.

Friday night came.

About ten o'clock I prayed, "Lord, I'm as confused now as when I came to Chicago. I've wasted a week seeking Your will, and nothing has happened. It must be this isn't the time You wish to reveal a plan for me. I'm going to spend a little more time reading the Bible, then go to bed and return to Lima in the morning. I'm sorry for taking the attitude of commanding You to show me Your will.

I'll be content and wait until You choose the proper time."

A measure of peace came to my heart as I arose from my knees, picked up the Gideon Bible provided in the room, and sat down to read. I had been going through the New Testament and was now in the Book of Acts. I read with interest, trying to keep an open mind for any special counsel the Lord might have, but not anticipating any momentous discovery.

Chapter ten of Acts tells of the vision Peter had. Peter, like me, was a man of prejudice. He believed in the letter of the Old Testament law, that there were clean meats and unclean, and that the man who would please God must not touch the unclean. In this particular case God was molding Peter's attitude in respect to the Gentiles. Peter was a Jew, the chosen of God, the clean people. To him Gentiles were unclean, lost, beyond the grasp of the grace of God.

But then Peter had his transforming vision, a vision of *all manner of fourfooted beasts of the earth, and wild beasts, and creeping things, and fowls of the air. And there came a voice to him, Rise, Peter; kill, and eat. But Peter said, Not so, Lord; for I have never eaten any thing that is common or unclean. And the voice spoke unto him . . . What God has cleansed call thou not unclean.*

Unclean.

The motion picture!

Slowly closing the Bible, I began to think. Did this pertain to me? Because of my basic timidity had God been putting the suggestion of film evangelism into my thought as a crutch to help me develop boldness in witnessing? In my heart I consented it might be so, and the rebellion, the prejudice, began to melt in my mind. In its place came peace, assurance.

"I will do it, God," I whispered.

You know, the two most powerful words in the English language are those, **I will**. It is when we conform our will to the will of God that peace and meaning come to life.

I browsed further in the Scriptures, back across areas I had read previously during the week, and God personalized for me the words of Jesus in the fifteenth chapter of John, where He said, *You have not chosen me, but I have chosen you, and ordained you, that you should go and bring forth fruit, and that your fruit should remain; that whatsoever you shall ask of the Father in my name, He may give it to you.*

70

The breath of courage came to my heart. I would dare to witness, in the strength of Him who had chosen me to serve Him!

When my friends back in Lima heard of the plan they offered little encouragement.

"You're making a mistake, Stanley," they said.

"What about the Sunday school? We need you."

"You'll run out of prospects."

"Are you sure people will let you come into their homes just to show movies? Wouldn't it be better to invite them to attend church?"

I tried not to seem bullheaded about my convictions, but I was resolute, for I was sure this was the work, at least for now, God had for me to do.

Securing a projector and a couple of films which pointed up man's need for salvation and God's provision of redemption in Jesus Christ, I began to give thought as to people I might call on. With the help of our pastor and also from contacts made during my Sunday school work, I soon had a sizeable list. Selecting what seemed to me a family likely to be cooperative, I made the first telephone call.

To my delight they welcomed the idea.

I was pretty rusty at first. To be a soul-winner means to be able to speak unoffensively to people, to have a winsomeness and a genuineness which makes them want to have you help them. I wasn't blunt to people on those first encounters, but neither did I quite know how to bring them to a place of decision.

But one heartening situation characterized virtually every home visited. The people were on guard at first. They would tell me how good they were, how they really had never done anything to displease God, but as I showed them a film and as we talked, the defense mechanism would break down. What's more, these people accepted me as a friend. I wasn't some kind of religious nut to them. I was Stanley Tam, one of the businessmen in town, who had a deep assurance of God's presence in his life and was sharing it with others.

While I didn't lead anyone to positive commitment of his life to Christ in those first homes visited, I made friends with people who desperately wanted a Christian friend. Many of them began regularly attending our church, a number of whom took the all-important step of receiving Christ into their lives.

I'm convinced every Christian can be a soul-winner. Remember the Bible says, *One plants, another waters, but God gives the increase.* You may not be able to bring every person you contact to a knowledge of Christ, but you can plant the seed or nurture the seed. You can be a stepping stone. Only the Holy Spirit can bring a man to Christ. We are merely the tools used to carry the message.

I was very shy at first. Sometimes I did little more than chat with the people where I visited, inviting them to church, but experience is an able teacher, and with each visit I gained confidence.

My well-meaning friends had said I would run out of contacts. On the contrary, I was getting more homes to visit than I could schedule. First, I set aside Tuesday and Thursday nights, but it wasn't long until other appointments had to be made.

But I will never forget the first night of actual harvest.

It was a middle-class home. The father and mother were very friendly. The mother was a believer, the husband was not. I showed a film. I could sense how deeply the father was impressed. I prayed throughout the showing, earnestly, desperately.

When the showing was over and the lights turned back on, the father and I chatted for a few moments. I could see how intently his wife was praying even though she kept her eyes on us.

"Y'know," the man said, "I used to attend Sunday school regularly when I was a boy. Quote Bible verses? Say, I knew dozens of 'em. But it's a funny thing. In all those years of attending Sunday school, even church sometimes, nobody ever asked me if I wanted to be a Christian. If anybody had, I just might've become one. As it was, I sort of drifted away from the church."

My heart was pounding like a triphammer as I said, "You could take Christ into your life tonight just like you saw in the film."

He looked squarely at me, unflinching, wonder and hunger in his eyes.

"Why don't you do it, Frank?" his wife whispered.

He turned to her. He turned to me. "I just believe I will," he said.

That was the first one, a soul for whom Christ had died and whom I had been privileged to bring into His kingdom.

Soon there was another, then another, then more. A number of

72

these people began coming to our church. They gave evidence of transformation in their lives. It wasn't long until some of my most skeptical friends were suggesting homes I might visit.

Then on one of my rare evenings home the doorbell rang. It was a young man from our church.

"I was wondering," he said. "Well, I'm a little shy really, but I've got an awful burden on my heart to help people find God, and I was wondering if I could maybe use the projector on the nights you don't need it, and I was wondering too if maybe you'd give me some pointers on how to help people."

In a short while there were sixteen of us at church engaged in this exciting ministry of door-to-door evangelism.

Nowhere on earth can you find a sight to behold, a new taste to enjoy, an adventure to experience, that can begin to satisfy the heart like the joy of bringing people to a personal knowledge of the Son of God.

Too bad so many well-meaning but blundering and inept people have spoiled the image of personal evangelism. There is not a warmer act of friendship, not a more profound exploitation of human relations, than to politely and tactfully invite a man to Christ. If he isn't interested, don't bother him. I never embarrass people—never push the issue. Remembering that the Holy Spirit must be the one who brings a man to Christ, I only seek to be God's instrument, the tool the Holy Spirit uses to bring light into dark, seeking hearts.

It is a ministry in which every Christian can share!

11

You might say we got into the plastics business by accident.

Only I don't believe it. For by now you know how tenaciously I do believe that when a man seeks to center his life around an unbroken continuity of faith in God there are no such things as accidents. The Bible assures us *we know that all things work together for good to them that love God.*

Here's how it happened.

In 1955 we developed a new silver collector which required a larger container than had been formerly used. We looked around Lima, called a number of suppliers, but no one had what we needed. It felt a little like building a boat too big to take out of your basement.

Then while attending a photofinisher's convention, I strolled among the booths one afternoon and came upon an exhibitor displaying exactly what we needed, a three-and-a-half-gallon plastic bucket.

"These new?" I asked.

"Brand new," he replied. "Not even in the stores yet."

We talked prices. He gave me a good quantity quote. I ordered a large supply.

One of the buckets went out with each of our new collectors—routine, we thought. Photographers would simply pour their waste fix into the buckets so the new and larger silver collectors could get to work.

To our amazement photographers began writing and calling from all over the country, wanting to know if they could order extra buckets for their own use. Our stock dwindled. We ordered more, reordered repeatedly, selling hundreds of the new-type plastic containers.

One thing led to another. Did we have plastic tanks for sale? What about spigots? Plastic tubing? Did we have any other plastic goods available? Before long we were printing flyers about the various items in stock, stuffing the flyers in letters and billings.

"You know something?" I said to my wife one night. "This plastic business just might outgrow the silver division."

"Maybe that's God's provision," she said. "You've been a little concerned about what may happen to silver."

I read the paper a few moments. Juanita was mending some of the children's clothes. I got to thinking.

"Honey," I said.

My wife looked up.

"So much is happening in the business I get a little concerned."

"Why?"

"Well, you know, it's incredible all that's happened in these few years. I was just thinking again today. We pay cash for everything, haven't borrowed a cent since the twenty-five thousand dollar note to put up the first building. We're expanding our inventory and all of it is paid for."

"That's wonderful. You're a good business man, sweetheart, and I'm proud of you."

"I'm not so sure how good a business man I am."

"I'm sure." She smiled playfully.

"Seriously, Juanita. It's been hitting me harder than ever lately that our business is growing because of God's blessing, not because of my ability."

"What is it, then, that concerns you?"

"I keep wondering if I'm holding up my side of the responsibility."

She looked at me puzzled.

"Here's what I'm thinking," I explained. "What would you say if we called in one of these efficiency experts to go over our procedures with a fine-tooth comb and really analyze us from stem to stern?"

She made no comment.

"Of course, what bothers me is that if we really do seek God's guidance on every day's activity, on every project—"

"What you're saying is a business God runs doesn't need the counsel of an efficiency expert?"

"I guess so, except—"

"Except what?"

"Put it this way," I tried to explain. "I'm human. Though I try to follow God's guidance, I'm not immune to making mistakes."

Juanita looked at me but did not comment.

"It's the stewardship side that concerns me," I went on. "Every additional hundred dollars we can turn in profit means that much more we can give. I want to be sure I'm not doing things which might hinder profits. Nobody's pressuring me. We aren't running into any obvious problems of any sort. But the idea of getting some counsel has been on my heart for some reason."

"Maybe that's because you should do it," my wife said. "You've always been on your own. You don't have the usual type of corporation board for counsel. You never had a chance to pick up executive experience from an employer the way many men do. Maybe an efficiency expert could give some helpful suggestions."

So it was that a George S. May representative came to evaluate our corporation.

"I want you to be rough on us," I told him. "Don't pull any punches."

He went over the plant from the front lobby to the shipping dock. We showed him our billing procedure. He spent several hours nosing around our shipping department. He went over warehousing mechanics, reordering procedures, quality control, all aspects of customer services.

"You look to me like a pretty healthy operation," the efficiency expert said.

"Remember," I chided. "We want criticism."

He had a few observations such as more effective methods of invoicing, but nothing momentous.

I was a little disturbed as to why I had felt such a compulsion to have him come. Maybe it was because I knew we were in good operational form and wanted someone to give me a pat on the back. I'm not above such chicanery.

But then the May expert came up with a simple but great idea.

"It looks to me like you're missing a good thing in the plastics business," he said.

"What's that?" I asked.

"Well, you've been very careful in the selection of products—items with a good markup and fast turnover—but you promote these with a lot of unrelated leaflets. Why not get all this information together in an attractive catalog?"

This one suggestion has been worth hundreds of thousands of dollars, for our annual catalogue has become the bread-and-butter backbone of our entire operation!

In ten years the plastics division grew from just under fifteen thousand dollars per year to a multimillion dollar annual gross, and it's still growing.

Our initial corporation handling the silver business was organized as the States Smelting and Refining Corporation. But soon it became necessary to initiate a new corporation called United States Plastic.

The plastics business is a tremendous windfall, for we see an eventual termination of the silver industry. We place many of our collectors in hospital X-ray labs, for example, but now the trend is toward videotape instead of emulsion film. Similar innovations may take over in other areas of photography. But plastics in its field is the wave of the future.

Our growth has been so phenomenal that the Internal Revenue Service audited our books for ten consecutive years. As a matter of fact, the local IRS man told our lawyer his office averages about eight "squealer" letters each year from people who claim to have inside information proving we welch on taxes.

Last year we paid substantially over three hundred thousand dollars in taxes, and for the first time the IRS didn't come in to audit our books. Apparently, they at last believe us when we say this business belongs to God, and we operate it on Christian principles!

"You know, sweetheart," I said to my wife one day, "it's just the way the prophet Malachi put it. The more we give to God, the more He opens the storehouse of heaven and showers us with material blessing. If we hadn't turned fifty-one percent of the stock over to Him, I'm convinced that the one hundred percent profit we'd be making would be less than half of the forty-nine percent we now receive from the company."

We read Malachi's declaration at our family worship that evening. It is a call to every Christian—God's request to us, His ultimatum to Himself.

Bring you all the tithes into the storehouse, that there may be meat in my house, and prove me now herewith, says the Lord of hosts, if I will not open the windows of heaven, and pour out a blessing, that there shall not be room enough to receive it.

Profits going into our charitable foundation, in spite of the high amount of taxes paid to the government, made it possible for us to dispense increasingly larger sums of money for Christian service mostly to missionaries and for projects overseas.

Because of this we decided that year, 1955, to take a trip to South America, visiting Ecuador, Peru, Brazil, and Colombia.

It was on this trip that I was to face a crisis I could not have remotely anticipated the day when in a lonely hotel room I told God He could have every bit of me—my life, my talents, my future, everything.

12

The prelude to our South America trip occurred three years earlier in January of 1952, when an evangelist by the name of Dwight Ferguson came to Lima for a two-week crusade sponsored by our church. Though participating on the steering committee, I had never heard of this man and, being quite busy, complained a bit to my wife about our evenings being tied up for so long a time.

But this was no ordinary man.

For the opening nights he spoke only to Christians. He did not follow the usual procedure of haranguing church members to shreds, but with power and compassion he expounded from the Scriptures the place of the Holy Spirit in the life of a believer.

On the fifth night I went to the altar. Pride had crept into my life, complacency, self-satisfaction. I asked God to empty me of self, of pride, and to let the Holy Spirit fully control my mind and body.

It was a time of dynamic renewal in my Christian experience.

The speaker and I became close friends, and as the conclusion of the meetings drew near, he startled me by saying he planned a trip to Formosa, Korea, and Japan, and wanted me to go along to give my testimony as a Christian businessman.

Having never before left my business or my family longer than a week, I didn't take the idea seriously.

But after he left Lima, Dr. Ferguson wrote to me every week

urging me to begin making plans. My wife and I talked it over many times, wondering if this man was merely being persistent or if it might be God's will for me to go.

"Our stewardship emphasis is on missionary work," Juanita reasoned. "If you had business interests in the Orient you'd go to check on them. Maybe this trip will help you better understand our giving responsibilities."

"You make it sound like I don't have an alternative."

"I wouldn't say that."

"But you think I should go?"

"Selfishly I don't, but I wouldn't lift a finger to discourage you if you felt sure it was God's will for you."

"Okay, let's put it this way. I'll plan to go unless something happens to make the trip impossible."

What a decision!

My grandmother died. Six days later my father died. Then my secretary who had been with me ten years and was indispensible to operating the business when I was away notified me that her husband had taken a job in another city so she would be leaving.

I told Dr. Ferguson not to count on me.

"It is vitally important for you to go," he wrote in reply. "God has given you the gift of being able to express yourself to other laymen. There is a vital need in missions today for laymen who can stimulate others in the task of world evangelism."

I didn't answer his letter.

A week later he wrote again. "I'm praying for you. I believe the Lord is going to help you clear matters so you can go."

I still didn't answer.

Dr. Ferguson kept writing. I've never met a man more persistent. Or more persuasive.

It got so I dreaded to see his letterhead in my mail.

Summer came and he wrote to tell me he would be speaking at the Winona Lake conference grounds.

"I'd like to hear him again," Juanita said.

"So would I," I told her, "but I also need to convince him how out of the question it is for me to think of a trip to the Orient."

Dr. Ferguson introduced me to several missionaries, talked profusely about the coming itinerary, and never did give me a chance to turn him down flatly.

Returning to Lima, I told my foreman the trip was off. To my amazement he looked at me almost as if he were the boss and I the employee and said, "You'd better go."

My wife's reaction was, "I've felt for a long time you should take the trip."

That night I wrestled for several hours with the problem, finally saying, "Lord, if you really want me to go, I'll go."

In that instant a liberating peace came over me.

"We'd better get busy," I told my wife. "I've only got a few weeks to train a new secretary."

There was an exceptionally well-qualified Christian girl we had tried to hire before but couldn't. We decided to try again.

"I'm sorry," she said. "I like my present job. It's downtown where I can meet several of my other friends at lunch. It's on the direct bus line home. If I worked for you I'd have to transfer."

We continued searching. It seemed fruitless. Good secretaries are hard to come by.

"Maybe this is our answer," I told my wife. "Like Abraham and Isaac. I tell God I'll go, and He shows me I don't have to."

"What are you going to do?" Juanita asked.

"Tell Dr. Ferguson I can't get away."

Then I got a telephone call from the first girl. "Is that job still open?" she asked.

I told her it was.

"I haven't been able to sleep," she said. "God has been telling me I shouldn't have turned you down, and I've tried to give every excuse I could think of, but last night I told the Lord I'd take the job if it was still open, and it's the first peace I've known in days."

The last week of September I headed west across the Pacific with the relentless Dwight Ferguson.

I'll never forget the flight.

Dr. Ferguson is a most amiable man, warmly human, engagingly genuine. He has the gift of motivating and molding people by helping them recognize their latent potentials.

He encouraged me to look for widening opportunities to stimulate laymen in the full stewardship of their lives.

I looked forward to our weeks together with increasing anticipation, but just as we arrived in Formosa Dr. Ferguson received a cable from his wife. Their son had been killed in a hunting accident.

"I feel I must go back," he told me.

I agreed he should.

"You can take my itinerary for me," he added.

"I?"

It staggered me.

"Just give your testimony, Stanley. Tell people what God has done in your life. That could mean a lot more than my preaching."

I tried to argue. He listened, unpersuaded.

"There has been a heavy burden on my heart ever since we met at your church in Lima," he said. "I've felt you had to be on this trip for the sake of your own future and the future of foreign missions."

I didn't understand.

"It keeps coming to me," he continued, "more forcefully each time I think about it—how effective you could be stimulating laymen to get behind the work missionaries do."

"In what way?" I asked. "I couldn't leave my business."

"You wouldn't need to."

With several other missionaries I saw Dr. Ferguson off on his plane. It was a strangely unnerving experience to watch the ship take off and gain altitude and head toward the horizon.

That night I had my first appointment as the bereaved father's stand-in.

Fear drove a cold-hot knife into me as I stepped to the lectern. I prayed for courage and strength and the right words to say.

It was rough.

After my first message I turned to the interpreter, a Chinese pastor, and asked, "Do you suppose the people got anything out of what I said?"

He bowed politely and in a voice laboring to be kind said, "Mr. Tam, perhaps you could try to do a little better next time."

It was plain to see that people were disappointed as I struggled from place to place, trying to fill Dr. Ferguson's shoes.

We came to one church badly split by inner schism. Half the congregation catered to one mission board, half to another. It was like walking into a mausoleum.

As I prepared for the third message, God laid upon my heart a simple equation: "Nothing plus God equals God." I put together some thoughts, giving a lot more time to prayer than to what I would say. I was desperate. I felt like a complete failure. Not that

I had to succeed as a speaker, but I felt I was failing my Lord.

God blessed that message, and a cleansing, empowering spirit of renewal came to the congregation. It was one of the great experiences of my life.

I understood the reason some days later when I received a letter from my wife in which she wrote, "When we heard of the tragedy in Dr. Ferguson's family and realized you would be left to fill his appointments, our entire church went to prayer for you."

The news had come to Lima on November 7th, the same day I spoke on the subject, "Nothing Plus God Equals God."

I have an undergirding confidence in the power of prayer. Don't ask me to explain prayer, for I can't. God who sees and knows all about us can intervene in our affairs. He often does. But He also listens for the sound of our admission of need. It is somehow a part of His personality as God to want to hear us praise Him and ask for help, and in response, for Him to bless us and intervene at the time of need.

True, many people tell of flamboyant experiences when spectacular answers came in answer to prayer. I have heard of instances so out of the ordinary I frankly dare neither deny nor affirm them. I only know that God is good, and our nothingness makes His omnipotence the more obvious. And in my own experience I know it has been the quiet evidences—the supply of guidance, of wisdom, of added strength—which most solidly affirm for me the reality of prayer.

Too many people who rarely pray otherwise turn to God for help in time of stress and calamity. Often God answers out of His heart of love. But it is the daily walk with God, the give and take of communion with Him which gives prayer its fullest meaning. Now you might say, in the case of my need in the Orient, people began to pray because of the stress emphasis, but I don't think this was the reason. The people at our church are human beings given to virtues and foibles the same as any sample segment of society. The differences lies in their spiritual transformation. Faith is vital to them because it bedrocks their lives through their relationship to Christ. Also, they think in terms of witness, of God's direction, of opportunities to serve. And so when my wife told them how Dr. Ferguson's situation left me with the responsibility for filling his itinerary, my friends began to pray God would use me.

And God delights to hear and answer the "use me" kind of prayer!

"We are not only praying for you," my wife wrote, "but we are convinced God knew the future, and the reason He laid it so strongly on Dr. Ferguson's heart to invite you was because this was to be such an important time of opportunity and growth in your own Christian experience. How tragic if you had insisted on staying home."

For the remainder of the trip everything was different. Missionaries opened their hearts to me. In churches and in auditoriums, wherever I gave my testimony, the Holy Spirit spoke to the hearts of those who listened.

In Korea Christians filled the churches wall-to-wall at five in the morning as they gathered to pray. For nightly meetings no advertising was necessary; no visitation program urging people to come. Simply turn on the lights in the church auditorium, and in half an hour it would be packed to capacity. It was a bonanza for an unknown American laymen. You don't promote meetings in Korea on the basis of who the speaker is. People come because they believe Jesus meant what He said when He promised us, *Where two or three are gathered together in my name, there am I in the midst of them.*

Those dear people ministered to me more than I did to them.

It was in Korea that one of the verses of the Bible leaped, as it were, from the page and burned its way, never to be erased, into my heart. I will share the experience with you, but first let me tell you of a special privilege God gave me on the plane from Seoul to Tokyo. We were about midway in the flight when I went to the washroom. Returning I saw someone had taken my seat. Since the plane was not crowded, I said nothing but selected another place.

I sat on the aisle. A Korean sat at the window. I thought to speak to him but supposed he would only point to his mouth and ears indicating he could neither speak nor understand English.

Then on an impulse I said, "Hello."

He returned the greeting in nearly flawless English.

"Where did you learn to speak so well?" I asked.

He replied, "When I was young my father told me if I would learn to speak English I would never need to worry about making money, so I went to Shanghai and studied. Now I am a businessman, and I find what my father said is true."

"I also am a businessman," I told him.

"Do you have your own company?"

"Yes," I replied.

"You are the sole owner?"

"It is a partnership."

"Are you the senior partner?"

"No, my partner has the control of the business. He is a very wonderful person. I would like to tell you about Him."

"Oh yes, indeed," said my new Korean friend, "tell me about your partner."

I told him. He listened eagerly.

"That is a wonderful thing," he told me. "You see, I too am a Christian."

"That's wonderful!" I exclaimed. "I met so many wonderful Christians in your country, I should have surmised you might be among them. I'm interested to know how you became a Christian."

"Well," he said, "it's like this. I have an uncle in Korea who is a Christian. I have admired his life for many years, and I decided I would be a Christian too, just like my uncle. I thought about it a very long time. One night, seated at my home, I decided how to do it. I am a wealthy man, but I have many poor relatives. Some of them are very poor. I decided to invite these poor relatives to come live at my home. I told them to come and I would take care of them. I would give them a place to live. I would give them food and clothes. I am also sending their children to school. So you see, Mr. Tam, that is how I became a Christian."

Breathing a prayer for guidance I said, "Mr. Tsung, it's wonderful to meet a man with such a generous heart and a man who has such a great desire to know God. I can surely see it is no accident we met on this plane. I have my Bible with me. Could we read some of it together and share what it really means to turn from our sins and become a child of God?"

"That I would like very much to do," he said.

We spent several minutes with my Bible as I tried tactfully to share with him the words of salvation.

"Here is an interesting verse," I said turning to Isaiah. "Would you like to read it?"

"*We are all as an unclean thing,*" he read, "*and all our righteousness are as filthy rags.*"

I turned to the book of Ephesians. "Have you ever noticed this verse?" I asked.

"*For by grace are you saved, through faith,*" Mr. Tsung read, *"and that not of yourself, it is the gift of God; not of works lest anyone should boast."*

"Isn't it interesting, Mr. Tsung, how carefully God shows us that, no matter how much good we do on this earth, we cannot make ourselves good enough for heaven? This is why Jesus came into the world. The Bible tells us. *Christ Jesus came into the world to save sinners, of whom I am chief."*

I saw the evidence of spiritual hunger come deeply into his eyes.

"May I ask, Mr. Tsung, if you have ever received the Lord Jesus Christ as your Savior in the way the Bible so clearly shows us here?"

"No, Mr. Tam, I haven't."

"Would you like to?"

"Something tells me this is what I need to do," he said.

We bowed our heads as it became my honor and privilege to guide him into the first step of the Christian faith, personally receiving Christ into his heart.

We parted at Haneda Airport outside Tokyo. But three days later as I stood in line at a bank to pick up some money, I discovered Mr. Tsung ahead of me.

"Would you like to come with me to a Christian service tonight?" I asked.

"Very gladly," he replied.

To my delight he not only attended the service but gave his testimony, clear and unmistakable, telling of his new faith. When I returned to the states some weeks later, he sent me a letter.

"My wife would also like to become the right kind of Christian," he wrote. "Would you please send me some advice how to tell her? She wants to have the same peace in her heart I have in mine."

I wrote immediately.

A few weeks later a second letter came with a ten dollar bill in it. "Please send to me all the Christian literature this money will pay for," Mr. Tsung wrote.

This engaging Korean man became a symbol of blessing to the entire trip.

In Hong Kong I stayed at the beautiful International Hotel in downtown Kowloon. One day while waiting in the lobby for a missionary to pick me up and take me to one of the schools, a bellhop stepped up and politely asked, "Sir, what is that book you hold in your hand?"

"It's a Bible," I told him.

He looked at the book curiously, and I wondered if he had any concept of God or His word.

So I said, "This is God's book. In it He gives us the secret to eternal life."

He asked a couple of questions. Two other bellhops joined us. We got into a lively discussion about the Bible and the Christian faith. I did not mention Buddhism or any of the other religions of the Orient but tried to make positive statements about God's intervention in the lives of those who trust Him.

My missionary friend came, and I had to excuse myself. But I took out the little magazine reprint of my testimony and gave it to the boys. As I walked out the lobby door, I glanced back and saw them avidly reading.

"I'm going to try to talk to those bellhops some more," I said to the missionary. "They seem quite interested."

But I didn't arrive back to the hotel until very late. Other bellhops were on duty. I went to my room.

As I prepared to retire the telephone rang.

It was the hotel manager. "I'm sorry to disturb you at this hour, Mr. Tam," he said, "but could you possibly come to my office right away?"

"Is there some emergency?" I asked.

"No emergency," he replied, "but I must see you."

"I've retired," I said.

"Oh, sorry."

"But—"

"Could you come first thing in the morning then? It will be fine if I see you at breakfast time."

I presented myself at his office the next morning.

Taking a copy of my testimony from his pocket he said, "One of the bellhops gave this to me. I have read it with much interest. I see you are a businessman from America and have had many interesting experiences. Would you talk to my employees and tell them more about what is printed on this paper?"

I was dumbfounded and overjoyed.

"I do not want to impose upon you," he began to apologize.

"Not at all!" I broke in, coming fully back to my senses. "I'd be delighted to do it!"

I told him I had appointments in the morning but could be back in the midafternoon. We set three o'clock as the hour.

To my amazement I found he had gathered some sixty people in the dining room.

"We don't have this many employees," the manager explained, "but we have this many chairs, so I took the liberty of inviting some others as well!"

With the hotel manager serving as my interpreter, I had the privilege of telling those people what Christ had done in my life.

Next morning when I went to the check-out desk, the clerk showed me the bill. Across the bottom the hotel manager had written: *Paid in Full.*

The bellhop who took my bags to the door was the same boy who had initiated the lobby conversation. When I offered him a tip, he held out his hand in protest and said, "I cannot take a tip, sir. I am the one who is indebted to you for showing me the way to Jesus."

Now I began to understand the meaning of the Bible verse God had emblazoned upon my heart back in Korea: *Ask of me and I will give you the heathen for your inheritance.* It had come to me when I was among people who had suffered deeply as human beings and as Christians.

I had protested then. "This verse is for missionaries, isn't it, God?"

Yet the verse kept coming to my mind with increasing emphasis until on November 24, 1952, I underscored the passage in my Bible and prayed, "Lord, I claim this. I don't know why you give a layman such a verse. But I take it from You."

Beside that verse in my Bible I penned these words: "It is wonderful for a layman to be led by the Holy Spirit."

This experience stands as a definitive crossroads in my life. It is said few adults will substantially alter direction after the age of twenty-five. But the Christian needs to realize that one of his distinctives should be pliability. At whatever age we must be candidates for any change of course the Holy Spirit may designate.

My life was radically changed by the Bible verse God gave to me there in Korea. *The heathen for your inheritance!* I had, of course, read the second Psalm before. I had heard this verse. But prior to this trip I had been only nominally interested in foreign missions. Oh, I was interested, possibly more than a lot of Christians, but I had never really taken a stark and honest look at how lost our world is without Christ.

The heathen for your inheritance!

Those words clung to my thoughts throughout the remainder of the trip, and it was in Bangkok that the Holy Spirit confronted me with another concept, this also from the Psalms, from the heart of David as he cried out: *When I consider the heavens, the work of thy fingers, the moon and the stars, which thou hast ordained, what is man, that thou art mindful of him? . . . Thou madest him to have dominion over the works of thy hands: thou has put all things under his feet.*

These are strong words as to the place of man in God's creation!

Now I saw the full meaning. I could help touch a lost and dying world. And so I prayed, "Lord, I accept this challenge. Please help me now to run the business so we can make the kind of money that will help me really claim these promises!"

I felt like a soldier confident of victory.

But it was not until three years later, when my wife and I traveled to South America, that I faced the full implications of this new concept.

13

By 1950 our business had prospered to the point that we decided to increase stock controlled by the nonprofit Stanita Foundation to sixty percent. Being by nature a proud person, I suppose I yielded to moments of egotism. Deep in my heart, though, a spring of gratitude lifted heavenward, for life cannot offer us any more rewarding experience than to invest of ourselves and our means in the kingdom of our God.

Or so I thought.

During the next five years increasing opportunities came for speaking engagement—Rotarians, Kiwanians, Lions, the Holy Name Society, colleges, parent-teacher's organizations, and, of course, churches and summer youth camps. I prayed for the sense and wisdom to exalt Christ, not myself. God told the prophet Isaiah, *I am the Lord: that is my name: and my glory will I not give to another.* The Christian dare not consider those words idly!

Paul's exhortation to the church at Corinth contains another nugget concept basic to the enlightened utilization of our personal resources: *Who makes you different from another? And what do you have that you did not receive? Now if you received it, why do you glory as if you had not received it?*

Devastating, those words!

Who makes you different speaks of your physical characteristics. *What do you have that you did not receive,* speaks of your talents and abilities. Both come from God. Unquestionably then, many a

90

proud mortal will bow in contrite shame before God's judgment one day, having no answer to the question: *Now if you received it, why do you glory as if you had not received it?*

To be completely honest, I enjoy an audience, to see those who may have been skeptical or indifferent become moved by the Holy Spirit as God uses my testimony to touch another's heart. But I must continually guard against pride.

Surely God hates pride more than any other sin, apart from the rejection of His Son, and I suspect more men who have heard the Gospel refuse and neglect it as the result of pride more than for any other reason.

But a man can make a fetish out of humility.

We need to face up to our talents and abilities as well as our inabilities. Humility in itself is no virtue if it simply means we cower into the background and hide under a bushel the lights of service God has entrusted to us. In fact, humility of that stripe more often becomes a kind of pride, especially to the Christian who takes pains to make sure he is known for his humility. I believe a man can be outgoing, eager to use his talents for good causes, anxious to help people, in a sense someone in the public eye, and yet keep pride under control in his life.

That's really what humility adds up to, don't you think?—serving as a kind of safety valve on this stoked-up boiler which generates our pride.

I learned a lesson on this back in 1951.

The editor of a religious magazine stopped at my office and asked if he could interview me for a story on personal evangelism and house-to-house visitation. I agreed readily, and subsequently the magazine appeared. The editor had embellished the article with an impressive centerspread of pictures and copy all about this man Tam.

It was the first time I had ever been featured like this, and my eyes gloated over the material! It gave me an idea—why not run reprints and use them as handouts?

I said to a local printer, "Just photo the copy as it is, but I'd like to use a better picture of me."

"No problem," said the printer. "How many copies will you want?"

"Let's start with ten thousand."

So as I went on church-speaking appointments, a stack of these reprints would be left at the rear of the sanctuary with the invitation for people to help themselves.

"A wonderful idea," pastors told me. "Gives continuity to your ministry."

Many asked for additional copies to give to those not in attendance or for use in pastoral visitation.

I considered that reprint a master stroke and am sure I had many good intentions, often praying for God's blessing upon the printed testimony as it fell into the hands of those who had not heard me in person.

But then I began having conscience problems.

"Stanley," God spoke to me, "why do you pass out reprints of that magazine article?"

"It's my testimony, Lord. I want it to help people."

"But is that the real reason?"

"Your Word says, *he that wins souls is wise*," I argued, "and I want to encourage people to be better witnesses."

"But is this your first reason?"

Penetrating, searing conviction came to my heart. For I knew the real reason I had made those reprints. It was so people would know that a certain magazine thought enough of Stanley Tam to run a centerspread article about him. It was to foster the Tam image.

One Saturday morning, miserable at myself for this flagrant yielding to my insatiable ego, I drove to the plant, loaded up the testimonies, and took them to the city dump.

"Forgive me, God," I prayed. "Pride is a cancer, and I almost permitted it to eat away whatever effectiveness there may be to my testimony."

This became a crossroad in my life, a positive, and I came to look back upon the experience as an undergirding to my determination to be obedient to my Lord.

Three weeks later a shipping clerk came to my office.

"We're out of those instruction sheets for silver collectors," he said.

"We can't be," I told him. "There should be several thousand of them on the shelf."

"I looked, Mr. Tam. I was sure we had several thousand when I used some last month, but they're all gone."

"Come, I'll show you where they are."

On the way to the stockroom the clerk said, "All I can find is that testimony of yours."

I felt my cheeks go pale, then crimson.

I had taken out nearly ten thousand instruction sheets, thinking they were my testimony, and burned them at the city dump. The magazine reprints, some eight thousand of them, lay stacked on the shelf.

I was thoroughly humiliated.

"Lord," I prayed, "let me learn the full lesson you have for me here. Do crucify my pride. You have been so good to me, surrounding me with material and spiritual abundance. Don't let me glory in it. I'm so human. But let Your Word become increasingly vital in my life. Let me be able to say honestly, *God forbid that I should glory, save in the cross of our Lord Jesus Christ, by whom the world is crucified unto me, and I unto the world.*"

I was so disgusted with myself I couldn't even discuss the matter with my pastor, though he was an exceptionally good man who had given me much helpful counsel and inspiration.

I kept the matter in silence until one day an out-of-town Christian leader stopped by my office. We talked about various things, and then I told him my problem.

"Let me see one of those reprints," he said.

"I'm half ashamed to have you read it," I told him.

I watched him as he read. I wished I hadn't mentioned the matter to him.

Finishing he said, "There's nothing wrong with this. The problem was with you. From what you've told me, though, I take it you've settled with the Lord this matter of pride."

"I've certainly confessed my sin and am determined with God's help to not let this sort of complex happen again," I said.

"That being the case, I'd suggest you continue using the reprints. They should be helpful to lots of people. As a matter of fact, I'd like to have a quantity of them myself."

I took his advice and not only distributed the remainder of those leaflets but also have reprinted the story many times since. My Lord used it to open the door for me to witness to those staff members of the International Hotel when I passed through Hong Kong.

Telling others about God's goodness in my life has become almost my first occupation. No small measure of His blessing has been in the provision of a faithful and capable crew working in our plant. Many of them consider themselves special stewards of the Lord's goods, just as do my wife and I. And certainly, as someone once put it, for the Christian there should be no differentiation between spiritual and secular. Everything about us should be so related to Christ that even the driving of a nail becomes an act of service done in His name.

Since we are in the mail-order business, much of our operation boils down to routines. This in itself helps make my speaking itineraries feasible. But the best of routines fall apart without good management, and this we have in our business. Earl Gaskill has been with us since the early days of operation. He's plant manager. Peter Courlas is our office manager. We talk nuts and bolts in our sessions together, because there's a lot happening in our business; but though these men operate as effectively as if the business belonged to them, what thrills my heart is the way they share with me in our spiritual objectives. Pete and Earl want us to operate efficiently and turn a good profit, because they're just as anxious as I am to produce more money for God's work.

Many times as I get up to speak I have the feeling these men and the many other dedicated workers in our place are standing with me.

Increasingly our emphasis is on missionary outreach. It's wonderful what God has done for us in our business—the opportunities we have as a business to reach out to confused hearts here in America—but we also remember the emphasis Jesus gave just before returning to heaven. He said we were to be witnesses not only in our home areas but also to the uttermost part of the earth. He didn't give us a choice of these areas but said our witness should include both.

I happen to believe strongly that one of the reasons our two corporations have prospered is not only because of giving God the profits but also because of directing so much of these profits into overseas work.

Though I am aware of the danger of sentimentalizing missions, of putting it out of perspective, I nonetheless feel God attaches a special importance to missionary activity. This was surely the case with the Apostle Paul's missionary journeys as he reached out to those who had never heard of Christ. Something happens in the heart of a Christian who really gets concerned about missionary activity.

God often makes demands of such a person which are not exacted from other Christians.

Such an experience was mine as the result of an invitation received in the autumn of 1954. It came from Christians south of the border asking me to speak in a number of churches and conferences.

January of the following year my wife and I went to Ecuador, Peru, Brazil, and Colombia, observing the work of missionaries, sharing our testimony with missionaries and Christian nationals.

But South America was to minister to me in multiples beyond any contribution of my own, as again and again the radiant witness of Latin Christians deeply stirred my heart.

Then in Medellin, Colombia, crisis came to my life.

The opportunity was given for me to bring the three concluding addresses at a series of revival meetings in one of the churches. On Saturday night a sparse crowd half-filled the sanctuary, but from the moment I began speaking I sensed a spiritual quantum different from anything I had ever experienced. Not knowing Spanish, I delivered my message through an interpreter, and it came forcefully to me that the missionary who related my words to the audience in their own tongue did so with unusual unction.

At the close of my talk I said, "God is present here tonight. He speaks with deep conviction to many of your hearts. Let us bow our heads. If the Lord has spoken to your heart tonight, slip out of your pew and come to the altar here at the front."

Immediately people began to come. There had been nothing emotional about my presentation except for urging those present to receive Christ and make Him central to their lives, but many were in tears. My wife attests that neither of us had ever seen anything quite like it before.

Nor since.

It was magnificiently spontaneous.

Usually, when a speaker concludes he sits down. I couldn't. I stood as though riveted.

For I came once again into a milestone encounter with God.

"What is the most important thing in all the world to you?" He said to me.

I looked down at the altar.

"To see people seek Your face, Lord, as a result of the Holy Spirit's blessing upon my testimony," my heart replied.

"Stanley, if a soul is the greatest value in all the world, then what investment can you make that will pay you the greatest dividends a hundred years from now?"

For a few moments it seemed as though I could project myself a hundred years into the future and from that vantage look back upon the panorama of my life. I saw the home I owned, the money in the bank, the investments I had in a couple of other companies, the plans I had for future earnings. I was giving God sixty percent of the profits from our business and doing exceedingly well with the forty percent coming to me.

"What are you asking me to do, Lord?" I prayed silently.

It was a precarious question to ask!

"Stanley," I could hear God's unmistakable voice in my thoughts. "If you agree a soul is the greatest value in the whole world and is the only investment you can make in this life that will pay dividends throughout eternity, would you be willing to go back to Ohio and become an employee of mine?"

"An employee, Lord? Isn't that what I am now?"

"We're partners now, Stanley. I want you to turn your entire business over to me!"

I was stunned.

"On the cross," I heard my Master saying, "I paid the supreme price that you might become My disciple. Are you willing to give all you have in order that others may come to know Me as you do?"

I bowed my head over the pulpit. Observers doubtless thought I was praying for those at the altar. At the moment, however, I was oblivious to those people, to the church, to the fact of being in South America.

I don't know how to explain the awe of that moment. I'm such an ordinary person. I make no claim to a special connection to heaven other than access available to any Christian. All I can say, and I mean it to glorify my Lord, is that when a man does seek to involve God at the center of his life, he can expect divine encounters.

A pragmatic streak runs through my normal thought patterns. I've told you I'm not a sentimentalist. But I have to insist I was dealing intimately with God those moments on that platform. If you doubt it, then I would like an explanation of why my own mind would generate a suggestion so completely at odds with my own selfish interests.

It had to be God!

He was asking me to turn my entire business over to Him!

It was incredible, beyond anything I had ever considered in the realm of stewardship and commitment.

Could I do it? The desk in my office wouldn't be mine anymore, nor even the pen used to sign my name. For nineteen years I had lived, eaten, and slept the business. I had gone through its birth pains, saw it now dawning into glowing success. A businessman thinks of his business every waking hour, plans a year or more in advance. It is his life, his security.

Now God asked me to turn it all over to Him.

"Okay, Lord," I managed to pray, loudly from the silence of my heart. "If this is what You want, I will obey. As a businessman I agree this is the wisest investment I can make."

I didn't tell anyone what had happened as moments later my attention came back to the humble little sanctuary.

"It was a wonderful meeting," my wife said when we were alone in our room.

I nodded.

"I was praying for you," she continued.

"Were you?"

"Of course I was!"

She looked at me inquiringly. I smiled, knowing she had not understood my question, but not at the moment offering an explanation.

I walked to the window and looked down into the street. A trio of Indian women sat complacently on the sidewalk in the light of a bright streetlamp, their backs against an adobe wall, chatting amicably about matters of the day. A farmer led his burro laden with bags of coffee beans. In contrast, a GMC truck snarled by, changing gears in anticipation of an approaching hill.

Whenever I see those of earth who are materially less fortunate, I breathe a prayer of gratitude. I prayed now as I looked on the street, but the prayer followed an alternate view.

"Something bothering you?" Juanita asked.

I didn't reply. She didn't press her curiosity further, and we retired.

I awakened early the next morning.

Frankly, I didn't feel very well.

After breakfast I took my Bible and slipped outdoors to some secluded trees.

"Lord," I prayed aloud, "I can't do it. I can't go back to Ohio and turn that business over to You. Isn't sixty percent enough? Many Christians don't so much as give You ten percent."

Even as I prayed, conviction returned to my heart.

"Perhaps it was an emotional decision I made last night, Lord."

The conviction grew stronger.

"Then You must show me definitely—give me a positive directive from the Bible. Please, God. Let me be absolutely sure."

I don't advocate the mystical procedure some suggest of getting answers from God by opening your Bible, putting a finger on a verse, and taking its contents as your directive.

Nevertheless, this morning I opened my Bible to the thirteenth chapter of Matthew's Gospel, verses forty-five and forty-six. *The kingdom of heaven is like unto a merchant seeking goodly pearls, who, when he had found one pearl of great price, went and sold all that he had, and bought it.*

That settled it!

And so on January 15, 1955, I told God I would no longer be a stockholder in either States Smelting and Refining Corporation or the United States Plastic Corporation.

All stock would belong to Him. I would be merely an employee.

My wife had been wonderful in the past when partial stock was delegated to our foundation, but my courage waned when I realized I must tell her of this final step. Not until several weeks later, one night after speaking in a church in Sao Paulo, Brazil, did I summon the courage.

She was wonderful.

Back home when we asked our lawyer to finalize arrangements —the same lawyer who had initially been willing only to alter my will—he said, "I will agree only on the condition you make your wife at least a part-time employee, to protect the two corporations in the event of your sudden death."

So my wife now handles payroll as well as other functions for which she is uniquely qualified.

En route home from South America I said to her, "Honey, if God is going to own the business we ought to give Him room to expand."

She agreed.

Don't misunderstand my wife. She has a will and a mind of her own. But she is also God's special gift to me, a woman who walks closely to her Lord and seeks to obey Him at all times.

That's a sure-fire formula for a successful marriage!

We had purchased property outside Lima, so we decided to build a new plant four times larger than the old one.

We decided to build the structure so that in itself it would give tactful and distinctive witness to our Lord. It stretches for two hundred feet along U. S. 30, the highway so integral to my earlier years as a traveling salesman. At one end we have three tall windows representing the Trinity—God the Father, Jesus Christ the Son, and the Holy Spirit. Next to the windows, in modern stainless steel lettering on solid stone, passers-by can read: CHRIST IS THE ANSWER.

Three posts on the canopy at the main entrance stand for the life, death, and resurrection of Christ. And inscribed on our cornerstone is the Bible quotation: *For other foundation can no man lay, than that is laid, which is Jesus Christ.*

I am convinced the business has just begun to grow.

And it is good, deeply and satisfyingly good, to know that the economic vigor of our coming years will all accrue, every dime, to the cause of Christ across the world.

So ironclad is our Stanita Foundation that two years ago our certified public accountant gave me a warning.

"You've been taking out the five percent contributions allotment the IRS allows corporations for donations. You may continue to do this, but it must not be given to the Stanita Foundation since the foundation owns the business and thus does not qualify to receive contributions from itself."

Which simply means as I said before, if Juanita and I were ever again to own our business, we would be compelled to buy back the stock certificates from our Heavenly Father!

14

A song we often sang in Sunday school went like this:

> Count your many blessings,
> Name them one by one,
> And it will surprise you
> What the Lord hath done.

One of the blessings that never ceases to amaze me is how, for those who sincerely seek to put Christ first, the day often seems to have a couple of extra hours.

Oh, to be sure, no one is really immune to the mad-rush psychosis of this modern world, but when our Master says, *"This is the way, walk ye in it,"* He has a way of helping us find time in every busy day for those things which must be done. There is always time for the important things—quiet searching of the Scriptures, meditation and prayer, touching the lives of those who come our way, meeting our normal responsibilities.

By normal responsibilities I'm thinking of family relationships.

The Christian who claims he's too busy serving God to look after his family is, in my opinion, too busy serving God. Not really, of course, because somehow in his well-intentioned service for the Lord he has permitted his life to get out of balance.

Juanita and I have four daughters—Rachel, Becky, Prudy, and Candy. What ministering angels these four precious lives have been to me!

Since God was not disposed to give us a son, more of the opportunity for influencing these young lives fell upon Juanita's shoulders. Yet for all my shortcomings, I've tried never to shortchange my family, however stringent my other time requirements.

When the girls were young, we romped about the living room together. I told them contrived stories, a little wild and woolly at times, but then all the more delightful to their adventure-seeking personalities. Even on nights I had to be away for community responsibilities I would try to delay leaving the house long enough for us to kneel together by their little beds, helping them learn the most important of all life's lessons—that of talking to God in detail about our needs and activities.

We did a lot of Bible memorization as a family. To me, a Christian who has not laid by a store of Bible verses is like a hunter with a gun but no shells.

One by one God permitted Juanita and me to help each of these dear little ones greet the dawn of faith. I feel sorry for Christian parents who relegate to the church the responsibility for the conversion of their children. The Bible says, *Train up a child in the way he should go, and when he is old, he will not depart from it.* Plainly to me, this means I not only have a responsibility to my children, but if I assume this responsibility, God guarantees the result.

Training up a child means first of all familiarizing him with the provision God has made for personal redemption, then leading him into the Christian life itself. In a measure this involves indoctrination. To me, however, the better word is training. And whether it is breaking a man in on a new job at the plant or any other kind of instruction, you cannot surpass the power of example. It is not enough to tell a child to trust Christ and live for His glory. A child must see the sense of it in your word and walk.

Friday night was family night, particularly when the girls were young. Juanita made candy and popcorn, and I got out the projector and showed films. The girls loved Mickey Mouse, especially when I ran the print backward. We played games, shared experiences, laughed, and sang. I wondered sometimes if I didn't look forward to Friday more than the youngsters did.

To my wife and me the choice of our summer vacation was of vital importance. We traveled from Maine to California, from Canada to the Gulf, and Juanita and I tried to see to it that getting there was half the fun.

We emphasized missions in our home, praying for missionaries, talking about their work. The children didn't always understand, especially when they were younger, I remember when Rachel got a little mixed up about the foreign fields as she prayed, "And, God, please bless the missionaries in the corn fields." Another time it was, "Bless the Chinese in Africa."

We insisted upon discipline. The girls think we may have been a bit too strict at times. Rachel says, "Since I was the oldest, Dad and Mom learned on me. I had an awfully hard time understanding why they were so strict about some things."

We had a "paddle stick" in the basement. Whenever its use became necessary, I went to the basement and began to count. The number of strokes was determined by how far I could count before the errant child arrived for punishment.

I make no claim of being a perfect disciplinarian. I can only say I tried. And it was always my concern to combine discipline with love and understanding. Juanita and I never punished the children without first sitting down and explaining to them the reason for the punishment. We tried, too, to take an active interest in the activities of the girls. I don't know what I would have done had I had a son who played football, because I'm not a sports fan. But when two of the girls qualified for membership in the marching band, I made it a point to be in the stands.

Come to think of it, I did get a little excited now and then when Lima pushed the ball into opposition territory.

Parenthood is such a complicated responsibility, the world so full of change and variables, that one cannot hope for perfection. Children will be content if they see honesty and sincerity in the efforts of their parents. And the payoff comes when your efforts to live a valid example and teach the good way come to fruition in the life of your offspring.

For example, Rachel fell in love with a handsome four-year letterman on our high school football team, the son of one of our top employees. He was two years older than our daughter, so he was a college sophomore the year she finished high school, and that year the persuasive agnosticism of a couple of college profs drew him away from some of the beliefs of his earlier years.

"Jack's all mixed up," Rachel told me. "He doesn't believe in the authority of the Bible as God's word. He thinks the miracles of Jesus can be explained away. Will you talk to him?"

I talked to Jack several times. He listened. He was courteous. But he had set his mind. In a way, I appreciated his open honesty, because he cared greatly for Rachel and knew he might lose her.

"You just look at things differently than I do, sir," he told me. "I don't say the teachers at school are perfect, but they are men with tremendous intellects. They aren't out to destroy the Bible. They're trying to find the truth. And when they apply the modern scientific method to the Bible, it just doesn't weather the test."

"But are you sure the Bible has been given a fair test by these men?" I asked.

"Well, they don't claim to be Bible students."

"Do they give the Bible any consideration at all?"

"Oh, everybody knows the Bible is a good book. It's just that people have put it out of perspective."

I tried to reason with him. I couldn't.

Juanita and I were deeply troubled. Our daughter had a strong affinity for this fellow, but we couldn't see how we dared to allow the romance to go unchecked.

One day I said to Rachel, "Your mother and I have prayed much about your future. You know how concerned we are about your relationship to Jack. We're sending you to a Christian school this fall. You'll meet a lot of fine young fellows there."

Rachel didn't give us any static, but in her eyes I could see the flame for Jack would be slow dying.

Things quieted for several months. Then during the college's spiritual emphasis week in the spring, Rachel had a new encounter with God.

"I've told the Lord I want to turn my life over to Him the way you've done," she wrote. "I want His will to be done in every thing I do, in all my choices and actions."

Tears came to my eyes as I read.

Then suddenly my eyes went dry.

For the letter continued, "And please try to understand, Daddy, I know how concerned you've been about Jack and me. I've been concerned, too. But as I knelt at the altar in chapel, God spoke to me very clearly. I believe it is His will for me to marry Jack."

Juanita and I were at a loss as to what to do. We had tried carefully to teach our girls the importance of seeking God's will. Dare we now write to Rachel and question the validity of her search? Had God actually told her to marry the young skeptic?

What about our prayers for her to find a Christian boy friend at college?

It was distressing.

The day came when Jack called for an appointment to see my wife and me. I knew what he wanted.

"I've come to ask permission to marry Rachel," he said as Juanita and I sat with him in our living room.

"You honor us, Jack," I said. "But you know it wouldn't work. Rachel sincerely desires God's best in her life. You have turned away from your faith."

"Mr. Tam," Jack replied, looking me strongly eye-to-eye, "I respect Rachel's faith. I wouldn't do anything to hinder her in her desire to be a really worthwhile Christian. But I've done a lot of thinking the last few months. I know Rachel's been praying for me, too. It's really hit me how prejudiced people get against the Bible. They don't give it fair consideration. Well, I've taken a new look at the Bible, and I realize some of those profs were challenging my faith and giving me nothing in return. I've asked God to forgive me for my rebellion. I've turned back to Him."

A silent doxology rose from my heart!

Today Jack and Rachel have a son and daughter, and Jack is an avid student of the Greek New Testament.

Our second daughter chose Houghton College in New York, a decision which initiated the circumstance of my posing as Cupid in her life. It seems that one Christmas season I had a speaking engagement in Buffalo, New York, which is near Houghton, so I arranged to pick up Becky to take her home for the holidays. As is customary on college campuses, students look for rides with others going their way, and four fellows asked for a lift as far as Lima.

One of the chaps caught my eye. He appeared highly intelligent and had a believable spiritual warmth about him.

"What was his name again?" I asked Becky after we had discharged our cargo at the bus depot in our town.

"His name is Wes," Becky told me.

"Keep an eye on him," I advised.

"Why?"

"Just keep an eye on him."

She did.

May of the following year they began to date. They have since married and look forward to a teaching mission overseas.

When Becky was fifteen and Prudy, our third daughter, was fourteen, we arranged a summer itinerary for them among missionaries in South America. We wanted it to be a memorable experience, as any overseas trek would be to youngsters at that age, but also prayed that the impact of missions would touch their hearts and influence their thinking as to their own futures.

Juanita and I met them in Miami on their return.

I had visions of their being apprentice missionaries by this time, and it was plain to see that the trip had been a meaningful experience, but our girls are more the demure type, and I knew it would take some persuasion to encourage them to show their slides publicly and tell of their experiences.

As we were returning through Tennessee, Prudy spied a chair lift going up the mountain. Suddenly she forgot all about South America and exclaimed, "Oh Daddy, could we take a ride on it?"

My first impulse was to refuse, but I admit to the occasional weakness of innocuous indulgence. I got to thinking.

"Could we?" Prudy pleaded.

"All right," I said, "on one condition."

"What?"

"We'll go on the chair lift, Prudy, if you and Becky promise to accept every speaking engagement you receive back home."

The girls subsequently developed a skit to go along with their slides, and in their Latin American costumes appeared before over one hundred groups.

Prudy had been quite shy, but the trip to South America and the following public appearances gave a blossoming grace to her young life. She became a campus leader at Asbury College and is now married to a young man preparing to serve God as a medical missionary.

But, though some of the girls experienced times of shyness, Candy was our neighborhood ambassador. She makes friends easily and as a child went from house to house in our area informing the neighbors about all our affairs. By the age of eleven she could sew her own dresses and even had shown a talent for designing. She took up painting, became an excellent swimmer, and could ride a horse like Annie Oakley. She did everything with a whirl, so much so that the beleaguered officer who took her on her driver's test flunked her because she had driven too fast.

At first she took the boys pretty much for granted. Being so active and full of fun, she enjoyed enterin into sports activities more than thinking of pensive walks or secluded chats. One boy began showing attention to another girl, however, and Candy suddenly awoke to the fact that she cared about him. She wouldn't eat, couldn't sleep, became apathetic.

We talked about the problem.

"Let's trust the Lord to bring the two of you together."

Candy liked the idea. We decided to ask for an answer to our prayers in ten days. She was full of faith.

But in ten days the situation remained status quo. Candy lost hope.

"I'll continue to pray," I told her. "We want the Lord's will done, and we can always trust Him for that."

Five days later the boy's attentions were all for Candy.

It was a puppy love affair, to be sure, but of desperate importance to a young girl, and the episode drew us close to each other.

That closeness was to dissipate in the glare of another situation. Television.

I loathe it.

While homes in the neighborhood sprouted antennas we stayed with radio, a record player, and lots of good books and magazines.

Candy chafed at the situation and was not beyond sneaking to the neighbor's house for a half-hour of Howdy Doody or Roy Rogers, especially if I happened to be out of town.

It concerned Juanita.

"Wouldn't it be better to have television in our house where we can control its use," she said, "than to cause the temptation of sneaking somewhere else to see it?"

The thought of one of our children sneaking for any reason infuriated me.

"It's not sneaking as such, Stan," my wife interceded. "Think back to your own younger years. Would you have been content if an invention like television appeared and you had no chance to look at it?"

"Juanita," I declared, "we are not having a television set in this house!"

Candy had by this time become a lovely young lady, a good student, poised, with a warm spirit, having a commendable choice of friendships. I wanted to be as close to her as I had been to the other girls. But a gap came between us.

"Hi, Candy," I would greet her upon arriving home from work.

"Hi, Dad," she would return, always cheerful.

"Anything special happen at school today?"

"Nothing special."

"Got lots of homework to do?"

"A little."

That was the typical sum of our conversation.

"I just can't get close to Candy," I said to Juanita. "We seem to be drifting apart."

Wisely, my wife made little comment.

It bothered me. At the office, on planes flying to speaking engagements, tossing at night, I thought about this quiet but painful rift in my family relationship. I brought special gifts to Candy. When I called home, I always asked about her. If she answered the phone, I would try to strike up a conversation, but she invariably turned the receiver over to her mother.

What could I do?

The answer was really quite simple. I could buy a television set.

But hadn't I provided every possible good influence for our girls? We didn't sit around and do nothing but read the Bible in our home. What about those stories I used to tell? Wasn't our house a house of books? We had given our children a reader's appetite for the classics. Why, then, stoop to television?

Candy is clever. At dinner she would sometimes mention outstanding programs her friends had seen and had mentioned at school. I tried to be nonchalant, even friendly.

But I did not want television in our house.

One evening, wrestling with the problem, I tried to put it once and forever out of my mind. Of course, I wanted to be considerate to my daughter. Under no circumstances must I bribe her for her love. As a matter of policy, I refused to buy anyone's loyalty. Then, too, hadn't I spoken out against the "evil box," as I called it?

Right there was where I got hung up.

Did I have a valid conviction or might this be another of Stanley Tam's dogged prejudices?

"Please, God," I prayed, desperate for wisdom on the matter, "show me what to do. If I am to stand against the modern tide, if television is not to be in our house, please give me direction. Give me peace in the matter."

God answered that prayer.

He gave me peace.

I went home early the next afternoon wishing to be there when our daughter returned from school.

Felicitations were as usual.

"Hi, Candy."

"Hi, Dad."

"Good day at school?"

"Yes."

"Any news? Anything special happen?"

"No."

I breathed a prayer to be sure I was doing the right thing. Candy started upstairs to her room.

"Say, Candy!" I called out.

She paused.

"Got a few minutes?"

She did not reply.

I could see Juanita in the kitchen doorway, watching, listening.

"I thought the three of us would eat out tonight," I said.

"Oh," Candy reacted.

"That okay with you?"

"Sure."

We went to a downtown restaurant. I was frankly a little nervous. We made small talk through the meal.

Again and again I breathed a prayer for guidance.

"Candy," I began as we waited for dessert. I cleared my throat. "I love you very much. I don't have to tell you something has come between you and me. We both know it. We both know what it is."

My daughter looked at me, her eyes intent.

"I want to apologize for being so outspoken about television," I continued. "I can't apologize for my views, because they haven't changed, but I'm sorry I tried to push my ideas onto you instead of giving you a chance to evaluate and make your own decisions.

"To me, television is one of the great spiritual hindrances of our day. To me, it's one of those 'besetting weights' the Bible talks about. Now, of course, I know there are good things on television. But I also know it's a thief. It steals valuable time from tens of thousands of Christians who ought to be serving the Lord instead of pleasing themselves watching a lot of silly programs. It's not only a thief but a killer destroying the sensitivity of the conscience for a lot of people, making sin look attractive. I could go on, Candy, but I don't want to make a big issue out of this.

"I've been tempted to go out and get a set for you. But I can't be guilty of trying to buy your love and loyalty. You wouldn't want me to stoop to that. What I do want is for you to keep on showing the perception you've shown as a young Christian. You're a wonderful girl, Candy. I'm proud of you. You may never have all the ideas about things that I have, but I know you'll be a Christian who really does try to put Christ first in her life.

"We're buying a television set for your room, Candy. All I ask is that you try not to let it stand between you and the wonderful progress you're showing as a young maturing Christian."

So now we have a television set, and things are the way they used to be between Candy and me. I didn't "buy" her loyalty that day. Rather, I said thanks to her for being such a good girl, for showing good sense and discernments, for endeavoring in her young way to be genuinely Christian.

I've asked God to help me think clearly about TV. But I still loathe the instrument. I've seen it take priority in so many Christian's lives. I just don't trust myself to risk having it take slices out of mine. Call me old-fashioned if you must, but I believe these are days when evil forces are in battle formation against the cause of Christ. I must not allow anything to deter my efforts for Him.

I do want to be objective. Perhaps Juanita and I have been too strict with our girls. We're very human. We've made our share of mistakes. But in the maturing lives of our children we see spiritual evidences which make us grateful to God.

And when I see what is happening to the American home today, including the Christian home, I wonder if we were really very far wrong after all.

15

Dear Mr. Tam:

> You are familiar with our organization and its
> ministry, and so I am sure you will look with
> favor upon the contents of this letter. I, as do
> many Christian leaders in America today, rejoice
> in the remarkable way the Lord has led and
> used you, and because of this I write to you in
> special confidence that you will look favorably
> upon my request. We have an urgent need for
> ten thousand dollars in our ministry. . . .

Letters similar to the above excerpt come to my desk in relentless
profusion, many from reputable individuals and organizations, and
I would like to help all of them.

But stewardship is a special responsibility between a man and
his God. A good steward is not one who has a given sum of money
to dispense and then waits for people to tell him where to dispose of
it. No, a good steward is a man to whom God has entrusted time
and materials, a man who subsequently looks to God Himself for
direction as to the best utilization of that which he has to give.

The Stanita Foundation annually distributes large sums of money,
but if I were to respond to each of the requests crossing my desk, it
would become necessary to break precedent and go to the bank
to borrow money.

Sometimes I receive a letter which states: "God has told us to ask you for five thousand dollars." My usual reply is: "While I certainly do not question your spiritual relationship, I can only tell you God has as yet indicated nothing to me about the sum of money you request, but if He does, you may be sure it will be forthcoming."

And I mean every word of it.

Some time ago a magazine in England ran a story about my work, and copies of this magazine were circulated in Liberia, with the result that forty letters came to my desk, mostly from Christian young people asking for funds. I remember one of the letters was addressed to Stanley Tam, Silver Refining, Ohio, USA.

Doubtless many of these young people are worthy Christians. Perhaps all of them. I cannot know. But I did not send funds to any of them, much as I may have wished to do so.

I suspect there are many Christians who never think about giving until the plate is passed at church or until someone comes along with an especially persuasive story.

I utterly reject such stewardship!

Our Lord is not a blind man with a tin cup. Giving to His cause is an investment, not charity. His Word says *it is required in stewards that a man be found faithful.* That means every Christian, whether he has a mite or a million to give, must carefully seek God's guidance in respect to his disbursements.

Three trustees shepherd the responsibilities of the Stanita Foundation. Each year as profits become available from States Smelting and Refining Corporation and from United States Plastic Corporation, we carefully seek God's guidance, asking Him to show us how best to dispense these funds. To His glory I can tell you we support more than twenty foreign missionaries. We have a special interest in Christian education of nationals overseas. Virtually without exception, then, we dispense the funds of the Stanita Foundation to these kind of projects—projects which we have personally sought out, projects about which we have carefully asked for the Lord's guidance.

Doubtless we make mistakes. But I'll tell you something. If every Christian in the world today would pray, "Lord, show me Your will in this matter of stewardship," the problem of financing Christian enterprises would immediately come to an end.

Stewardship, however, is a lot more than being able to put a given sum into the offering plate. Stewardship involves attitude.

111

Sometimes young businessmen come to me and say, "Mr. Tam, I'm deeply impressed by your story. My business is young and struggling, but I'd be willing to do what you've done. How shall I proceed?"

My usual reply is, "That's a wonderful attitude, and your willingness is the most important thing. But don't get your directions from me. Get them from God. If you want my advice, however, I'd say to go easy. Make sure you tithe, for that's the scriptural premise and the least you can do. Then, as the Lord prospers you, increase your giving to twelve or fifteen percent. If you continue to prosper, keep increasing the amount. The IRS, you know, allows you to give thirty percent of your personal income, though I'm afraid there are few Christians who ever consider taking advantage of this provision. But don't ever try simply to emulate another person. Obey God above everything else."

Then, too, stewardship involves the use of money. Frankly, I am not a sackcloth-and-ashes Christian. We have a modest but comfortable home. My wife and I dress well. We are careful with money, never lavish in our spending, and my daughters will tell you how I have urged them from childhood to think twice before making an expenditure to be sure they get the best value from their money.

It is characteristic of Americans—too often including American Christians—to adjust their living standards to their amount of income, usually keeping the former just a bit higher than the latter. But really, in this land which offers so much, where the poorest family in almost any community has more than the wealthiest family in some overseas areas I have visited, the thinking Christian needs to consider carefully that point at which he will be willing to say, "It is good enough."

I think, too, stewardship involves our very concept of what money is and how it should be used.

As a young Christian out on the road promoting the silver business, I would periodically tabulate my earnings and set aside ten percent for our church. On one occasion I had ten dollars to set aside.

Sunday morning came, the ushers passed the plates for our tithes and offerings, and I reached into my pocket for the envelope containing my contribution. It was gone.

Following the worship service I carefully retraced my steps to the parking lot, around my home, other places I could remember, but the money had disappeared.

Well, I told myself, it is really God who has lost the money. It belonged to Him. No one could blame me, for the loss had been completely unintentional. Was it not true that when I placed the money into the tithe envelope I had fulfilled my duty?

But the more I thought about it, the more I knew I was wrong. I owed God ten dollars. I lost the money before giving it to Him. It was up to me to cover that loss.

And so I did.

Through the years, and particularly those early years of the silver refining business, that decision has been like a foundation stone. Ten dollars was a large sum of money to me then, but the attitude confirmed by that experience has many times repaid the cost.

About this time God spoke to me concerning a pair of gloves taken from a Lima department store prior to my conversion, a pair of dress gloves worth seventy-eight cents. The more I thought about it, the more I knew I must make restitution.

"But that was before my conversion, Lord," I prayed. "Weren't all my sins covered by Christ's blood on the cross?"

I was willing enough to part with the money, but because of my shyness I was frightened at the thought of going to the store.

But I did it. I told the store manager what had happened in my life, and I'll never forget what he said. "Son," he told me, "I admire you for the step you have taken in your religious life. It shows character. I can assure you you have a bright future ahead of you."

You will remember my saying stewardship involves our time as well as our material means. That is, our use of time—attitudes, initiative, actions, and reactions—also comprises stewardship responsibility.

I have tried to establish five guideposts for my life.

1. To thank God for every adverse event.
2. Rather hold a bolt of lightning in my hand than to speak against a brother.
3. To pay any price in order to be obedient to the Holy Spirit.
4. To administer in love and never to govern in anger.
5. To pay three compliments every day.

Simple rules, to be sure, but they discipline me severely in my search for the ultimate in the good life.

You will note two items dealing with attitudes toward others in respect to times of stress. There is a special reason for this, since my Achilles heel happens to be an easily-triggered temper. Surely an unruly tongue and a tempestuous attitude writhe at the bottom of just about every personnel problem in the Church today.

During my years of Sunday school activity we had an especially fine pastor in our church. He was thoughtful, adept in handling people, but he also had a lot of drive and initiative. So do I. So it was perhaps humanly inevitable we should encounter misunderstanding.

On one occasion I stood up before the men of the church board and confessed a wrong attitude to this good man. It was an excruciating experience. But I was in the wrong. I knew it. There were only two alternatives—be stubborn and create a festering sore in our congregational relationships or be obedient to the Holy Spirit and make amends.

Several months after we completed our new building a man came into my office and said, "You owe my company five hundred dollars."

"What for?" I asked, surprised.

"We rented scaffolding to a subcontractor who worked on this building, but we never got paid."

"Why do you come to me?"

"He won't pay it."

"Then go to the general contractor who built this place. He's responsible."

"Not according to law," the visitor said. "Legally, the owner is liable, except we've waited too long to put a lien on the building."

I stood my ground. He became profane. I rebuked him for it, and he left my office boiling with anger.

Nine years went by. One day I drove past this man's place of business. The inner voice spoke to me with penetrating clarity reminding me I owed this fellow five hundred dollars.

"That's history, Lord," I argued. "The statute of limitations has made the bill void. Besides, I'm not the one who should pay it."

Yes, I was.

I fought the conviction for several days, then decided to go see the man.

"You remember that scaffolding used on our building?" I asked. He remembered.

"I've come to make restitution. How much do I owe you?"

The man's jaw sagged. He looked at me in disbelief. When he realized I meant business, he went to his file and looked up the account.

"It's been nine years," he said.

"I know."

"I'd be willing to settle for just about any amount. He wheeled around and faced me. "Give me two hundred bucks, and we'll call it square."

"I'll double that," I said. "I'll give you four hundred dollars." Whereupon I wrote out a check.

Moments later, leaving the building, I complimented myself. I had done more than he asked, but I had still saved a hundred dollars.

The next two days were misery. God spoke to me about the total amount, and I had no peace until I returned to the man's shop and paid the account in full.

We had some problems with our local post office, and a Negro employee was involved. So far as I am concerned, a man is a man regardless of his color, so pigmentation had nothing to do with this situation. It was simply a matter of my unleashing my tongue at this fellow because I didn't like the kind of service we were getting. I promised the Lord I would apologize next time I saw him, regardless of the circumstances, but I didn't see him again.

Months passed, and I forgot the incident.

But one day my telephone rang. It was the pastor of a Baptist church in our city. He was going to be out of town and wondered if I would fill his pulpit. Checking my date book, I found I had the Sunday free, so I agreed.

You've already guessed what happened.

The Sunday school superintendent was the man I had affronted at the post office!

I tried to get to him, but he was busy. Then, too, he well remembered the incident and was in no hurry for another confrontation. Time came for the worship service, and I was ushered to the pulpit. My heart pounded relentlessly. I knew I had no right to speak until I set things right with my Christian brother.

I was prepared to begin my message with that apology. As I

stood to speak, however, the man slipped out of the sanctuary. I cringed with embarrassment. I, of course, didn't blame him.

But supposing I had now been at least temporarily absolved of the need for saying anything, I began my message.

Then he returned. He had not left because of me but to look after one of his Sunday morning responsibilities.

I closed my Bible.

"Folks," I said, "I see your Sunday school superintendent has returned to the sanctuary, and before I try to say anything else, there's something I must make right."

The man looked up at me in surprise.

"Several months ago I wronged him at the post office where he works," I continued. "He knows what I mean, and before you people I want to apologize and ask his forgiveness."

Not only did this dear man forgive me and become in truth my brother, but a touch of heaven came to that meeting.

Was this some magnificent act of Christian virtue? No. I was simply doing what was right, performing normally as any Christian must do if he indeed determines to be obedient to his Lord.

I cannot overemphasize the importance of obedience. Only then can we be sure of God's blessing. Obedience not only means making restitution for flagrant sins but for the little things, *the little foxes that spoil the grapes,* as the Bible puts it. Many times I have had to apologize to my children when I spoke in anger instead of love. I have had to apologize to members of my staff at work.

If we walk in the light, as He is in the light, we have fellowship one with another, the Scripture tells us. *If we confess our sins, He is faithful and just to forgive us our sins, and to cleanse us from all unrighteousness. If we say that we have not sinned, we make Him a liar and His word is not in us.*

Let me share with you a simple formula for making sure you have no crossed wires in your Christian life.

The word to remember is *meditation.*

For it is in our quiet time with God when we ponder upon His words as recorded in the Bible, when we open our hearts for His surveillance, it is then the Holy Spirit points out those abrasions we need to look after.

Let me give you an example.

One year when we closed our books in the silver business, we made the surprising discovery that, according to our records, we had sold more silver bars than we had bought unrefined silver from our customers. It was a completely unintended oversight, a matter of our rating the silver we bought at a lower quality than we received when we smelted it into bars and marketed it.

It was the end of the year with Christmas in the air, and so I wrote the matter off as an innocent mistake, just one of those things. We were in a hurry to wrap up details at the office so Juanita and I could take the girls to Rockford for the annual visit to Grandmother's house.

One night other members of the family retired early, leaving me alone in the living room. I spent some time talking to God, and in my prayer I said, "Now, Lord, here it is almost the end of the year. I thank You for such a good year in the business. I thank You for the many ways You have helped us. It's time for inventory, Lord, and I want the Holy Spirit tonight to take inventory of my life. Please show me if there is anything in my life, whatever it might be, that needs to be made right before beginning the new year."

As I waited in the quiet, a voice whispered to my conscience, "Stanley, you have four thousand dollars that doesn't belong to you."

I hadn't been thinking about the silver sales, but I knew immediately what was wrong, for this was the amount we had underpaid the processing labs who used our Tamco collectors.

"Does it really matter, Lord?" I prayed. "We have three thousand customers. Four thousand dollars amounts to just a little over one dollar each. Surely that's only a routine error. It could happen to anyone."

"The four thousand dollars doesn't belong to you," the voice reminded. "It belongs to your customers."

"But they all send in different percentages," I argued. "It would be impossible to figure out three thousand refunds. It wouldn't be worth it."

The more I argued, however, the more forcefully I knew restitution must be made. It was God's command, and when He commands we have no sensible alternative to obedience.

We hired a special girl to do the work, and after six weeks she had the three thousand refunds ready to mail.

Then the Holy Spirit again spoke to my heart. Shouldn't I tell these customers why they were getting the money?

We printed a testimonial letter explaining that the impetus behind the refunds came from my personal relationship to the Son of God, telling how God had become my senior partner, how He had led us through the years, through times of insurmountable adversity, through times of growth and prosperity.

Because the refunds were small, I didn't anticipate any response. It really didn't matter. I had been obedient. That was enough.

We were deluged with letters, hundreds of them, commending us for this act. Many of those letters gave me an open door to follow through with my further witnessing.

In this case money was involved, but it was incidental to the deeper sense of stewardship. I didn't want to allot the time necessary to make these small repayments. Doubtless many a conscientious businessman would have felt it poor business procedure to do so.

But stewardship is more than money. It is obedience, constant listening for that quiet voice of divine guidance sure to be heard when we follow the precedent of the Word of God which says, *Whether therefore you eat or drink or whatsoever you do, do all to the glory of God.*

For that, you see, is what the Christian life is all about!

16

My contention that the Christian should have no secular interests because everything he does should be calculated to glorify God does not mean living a sanctimonious life, becoming so otherworldly that people look upon him as a curiosity rather than a valid human being. The whole point of God's craftsmanship in the making of a man is to keep him genuinely human and at the same time genuinely Christian.

There will be time enough to sprout wings when we get to heaven!

On the point of celestial wings and harps, it seems to me that many people have such sentimentalized opinions as to miss completely the significance of this life as a preparation for immortality. Heaven may have harps and streets of gold, but these will be incidental to the dynamic fulfillment of personality we shall experience when we see our Redeemer face to face and enter into eternal fellowship with Him.

And the wonderful things is that we can begin this relationship here and now!

The Apostle writes, *We see through a glass darkly; but then face to face; now I know in part; but then shall I know even as also I am known.* We can see the fullness of the divine now, he is telling us, but it is through a clouded window. To see the fullness of this reality we will need the eyes of our resurrected bodies.

Nonetheless there is the vision of Christ now, radiant and real and transforming, and we ought to use everything we do as a potential vehicle for sharing this vision with others.

Believing this, we have through the years sought to use our business as a means of witness. A tract has been placed in every shipment of merchandise for over thirty years and now we also include a page or two of testimony in the catalogue. In 1961, the year of our twenty-fifth anniversary, we utilized the silver theme as a means of getting out a special brochure of witness to our many constituents.

Let me caution you, however. If you decide to be more than a Sunday Christian, if you determine to represent your Lord on Monday through Saturday as well, then you put yourself on display in a highly demanding exhibition of the real you. People seem to cherish the word "hypocrite." It must surely be the largest word in the English language, because so many try to hide behind it. And, of course, the reason people speak of hypocrisy is for the most part a defense mechanism. But this does not relieve the committed Christian of his responsibility to make his life measure up to his witness—his walk and his talk, practicing what he preaches.

We stress service in our business. In the commercial world you are good to deal with if you pay your bills and give good service. Thus it goes without saying that service and fiscal integrity are prerequisites to using your business as a platform for witness.

We try. Hard.

But we make mistakes. We have problems with suppliers, especially those who promise delivery of plastic goods but rarely keep their promises.

"Hey, Tam!" a raucous voice will bellow at me on the telephone. "God is late again! You promised we'd have that shipment of tubing by Friday! It's Tuesday already!"

"I'm sorry. We called the supplier every day last week. We're having him drop ship to you as soon as he has the stock available."

"Instead of calling him, Tam, why didn't you just pray about it? Look, we've got to have that plastic tubing. You'd better scratch up a miracle and get it to us!"

"I'll do my best."

"Amen!"

I don't like that kind of phone call. Fortunately, it doesn't happen very often. When it does I feel more pity for the caller than embarrassment for myself. But such contacts are disciplinary, one among many reactions to our witness as an organization, challenging our effort to provide the ultimate in seller-buyer dependability.

The Bible tells us *the preaching of the Cross is to them that perish foolishness.* The Apostle Paul wrote to Galatia about the offense of the cross. Peter described Christ as *a rock of offense.* Thus while it is true that the uncommitted often look at our witness as an offense, we should nevertheless be acutely diligent to keep that witness from being unduly offensive.

Jesus said to His disciples, *Follow me, and I will make you to become fishers of men.* Now what is more important to a fisherman than anything else? Bait! He may have the latest rod and reel, a strong line, a bobber that looks as though it just fell through the rainbow, but he must have bait. This is what puzzles me so much about Christians who hesitate to use promotional principles in witnessing. I don't say we should walk around wearing a sandwich board—though if God tells you to do it, you'd better obey Him!— but I do feel we should use legitimate means to let hungry hearts know there is someone holding the pole, eager to help them find the peace and joy only Christ can give.

To me, the use of well-written, well-designed tracts is indispensable. Years ago a Christian photofinisher in Chicago challenged me to use these in our business communications when he told me he had placed over two million of them in orders processed by his company.

Shortly after we began doing this I received a letter from a darkroom man in a studio in Illinois. Fortunately, I had a forthcoming appointment in his area, so I put high on my agenda a stop at the studio where he worked.

"He's down in the darkroom," the proprietor told me. "It's in the basement."

I hurried down, found him washing some prints, and introduced myself. It was difficult to see in the dim light of the room, but I sensed his joy at realizing someone had come to help him.

"I've read that leaflet over and over," he said. "The more I read it, the more I want to find God, but I just don't seem to know how to do it."

"You want to do it now?" I asked.

"Can I?" he exclaimed.

"Right here in your darkroom," I assured him.

I took out my New Testament and stepped under the dim azure light. He joined me.

"Can you see to read?" I asked.

"Yeah, a man gets pretty used to the light down here."

We turned first to John 3:16, and he read those words of timeless magnificence: *For God so loved the world, that He gave His only begotten Son, that whosoever believeth on Him should not perish, but have everlasting life.* Then we turned to John 1:12, and he read: *As many as received Him, to them gave He the right to become the sons of God, even to them that believe on His name.*

Jesus said, *I am the light of the world; he that believes in me shall not walk in darkness, but shall have the light of life,* and this divine light flooded the darkness of the little room as my new friend bowed before God, confessing his sin, his emptiness, and asking Christ to cleanse his heart and control his life.

Until his death several years later we kept in contact, sharing many times of Christian fellowship.

Last year a photographer in Texas wrote, "I want to thank you for the leaflet you put in my shipment. Because of reading it I've become a Christian."

We know that many of these tracts terminate in somebody's wastebasket. Even in this, however, there can be a witness. I remember a photographer in our area who always threw our tracts away, but his daughter became ill, and the doctor told the man she would likely not live.

"I had just received a shipment," the father related, "and, as usual, I had thrown your literature into the wastebasket. But when the doctor warned my wife and me we might lose our daughter, I began to do some thinking about faith. I remembered the tract you sent and went to my wastebasket and dug it out."

He lived near Lima, so when he wrote and told me, I called and asked if we could get together. He readily agreed.

I went to see him several times. He was in deep distress. His daughter, a high school senior, kept losing ground. But he also looked at his own plight, and after several visits he opened his heart to the Savior.

Shortly afterward his daughter died.

I went to the funeral home praying the man would not become bitter and blame God for the loss of his child.

He met me at the door of the mortuary, gripped my hand and said, "It's okay, Stan. It's all right. If God wants my daughter, it's okay."

I still see him occasionally and thank God for the ring of genuiness which continues to characterize his faith.

A fellow named Bill Hains came into the plant one day and asked the receptionist if he could speak with the man who ran the business.

"He's back by the water cooler," the receptionist said, pointing me out.

Bill came to me, introduced himself, and said, "I'm from Sidney, Ohio. I was driving past your place and noticed the big sign CHRIST IS THE ANSWER. What does that mean?"

"Exactly what it says, Bill," I told him.

"Well, I belong to the Kiwanis in our city, and the fellows asked me to find a religious layman to speak for our Easter meeting, and when I drove past the plant and saw that sign—it's very attractive, by the way—I said to myself, now there's possibly a man who could speak to us."

We discussed dates for a moment.

Then I said, "Do I take it you are a Christian layman yourself, Bill?" I had reason to doubt it, which was why I asked.

"I don't guess I am," Bill said.

I saw hunger in his eyes so I asked, "Do you have a spiritual need?"

"Yeah," he said, "I sure do."

"Would you care to come into my office and share it with me? I'll help you if I can."

He agreed eagerly. We went into my office and closed the door.

"It's like this, Mr. Tam. Well, first of all, I'm a chain smoker, and it scares me with all this cancer talk. On top of that, I'm an alcoholic. I'm miserable. You know how it is, you're a salesman, and you can't do much business these days unless you buy the drinks and join in on the fun."

"I'm afraid I don't agree with that," I broke in, smiling, "but go ahead."

"Well, I'd like to kick both tobacco and alcohol. I've sure tried. Only, religion doesn't take with me somehow."

"What do you mean by that?"

"I belong to the biggest church in town. Everybody who's anybody goes there. I try to listen to the sermons. But nothing seems to fit my case. Well, there's this friend of mine at that church, and we got to talking once, and he invited me to the church he went to as a kid, a little church on the outskirts, and so we went one night, and the preacher preached hellfire and brimstone. It shook me up, and at the end of his sermon he asked any sinners who felt they needed to, to come to the altar, and I was the first one.

"They took me into a little side room and talked to me a bit and prayed with me, and I felt sort of good at the moment, I'll have to admit, but today I'm no different than I ever was. I drink like a pig. I light one fag off the end of the last one. I'm in bad shape."

I recognized the church of which he spoke, the one on the outskirts of his town, and knew it to be productively evangelical. I suspected the problem lay in his own heart.

After a silent prayer for guidance I felt inclined to ask, "Bill, do you believe the Bible is the Word of God?"

"Yes, sir," he replied, "I believe I do."

"You believe in heaven?"

"I sure do."

"Do you believe there's a personal devil?"

"A personal devil?"

I nodded.

He shook his head.

"You don't believe in a personal devil?" I probed.

"As a matter of fact, that's been discussed at this church where I'm a member, and the situation as I understand it, well, there's wrong in the world and all that, but—"

"You say you believe in heaven," I broke in. "What about hell?"

"Do I believe in it?"

I nodded.

"Well," he said, "I believe in it after a fashion, you might say. Now according to this church I attend, there's no literal place called hell, but a man can sure make hell for himself here on earth. That I believe."

"You said a moment ago you believed the Bible."

"That's right."

"You believe Jesus is the Son of God?"

"Oh, absolutely."

I reached for the Bible on my desk, opened it to the sixteenth chapter of Luke, pointed to verse nineteen and asked him to read.

"There was a certain rich man, which was clothed in purple and fine linen, and fared sumptiously every day; there was a certain beggar named Lazarus, which was laid at his gate, full of sores, and

desiring to be fed with the crumbs which fell from the rich man's table; moreover the dogs came and licked his sores. And it came to pass that the beggar died, and was carried to Abraham's bosom: the rich man also died, and was buried; and in hell he lifted up his eyes, being in torments. . . ."

Bill looked at me, his eyes questioning.

"Those are the words of Jesus you're reading," I reminded him. "Jesus is telling us about real men and real places. The rich man had died. His body was in the grave, but his soul was in hell, and he had all his senses. He could see, because he saw Abraham. He could talk, because he asked Abraham to send poor Lazarus and touch a drop of water to his burning tongue. He had senses. He felt the torments of hell."

"I sure never knew that was in the Bible," Bill said. "Never heard that portion mentioned at our church. I'm embarrassed. If the Bible says there's a hell beyond this life, I'll accept it."

I showed him pointed teachings in the Scriptures about the devil.

"You've got me on that point, too," he said.

"You know what your problem was in that little church your friend took you to?" I asked. "You recognized yourself as a sinner. That's why you went to the altar. But you were looking for reformation when you should have been looking for regeneration. You see, Christ can't save a man until that man admits he is lost."

Moments later I had the privilege of leading Bill Hains to a personal, transforming acceptance of Jesus Christ as his Savior and Lord.

Karl Bienke sold for a cardboard box company and called on me periodically for seven years. He was a wonderful fellow, active in his church and always anxious to discuss the Bible with me. I suspected, though, that Karl had a lot of knowledge about Christ, but when I would try to bring out the truth he would always out-talk me, and I make it a point never to pressure anyone on spiritual matters.

We prayed for Karl for many years.

One day he came to my office and, as bluntly as he had posed religious topics in the past, said, "Stan, you've got one thing I don't have, and I'd like you to tell me how I can get it."

Not sure if he was talking about something in the silver business or the plastics division, I said, "I'll do my best, Karl. What is it?"

"You've got assurance of eternal life," he said, "and I haven't, but that's what I need."

Joy sprang from my heart, sensing God's answer to our prayers of so many years.

"Karl," I said, "I'll tell you the position you're in. You're like a man who goes down to the automobile showroom and looks through the window at a new car. He likes the color. He likes the model. He likes the make. He's made up his mind it's the car he wants to buy, and he has the money in his pocket to pay for it. But instead of hunting up a salesman to consummate the transaction, he just keeps standing there looking at the car. In a way, as you have done with Christianity, he can claim it as his because he plans to buy it, only he never gets around to doing it."

He took me by the arm and said, "Let's make the transaction!"

We went into the conference room and over my Bible he confessed his sins, acknowledged Christ as his Savior, and received Him by his own personal commitment.

I'll never forget his prayer.

With tears streaming down his cheeks as he finished that prayer, he looked at me and said, "Why didn't I do this a long time ago?"

A good question!

Herb Speer came to the plant early one morning, his first visit, and was about to leave just as I arrived. He handed me his card. He was a paper salesman.

"I know your plant," I said, fingering his card. "Your prices are competitive, and if you'd gotten to us first, we'd no doubt buy from you. But we have an established source, and we're happy with it."

He thanked me and turned to leave, when the Holy Spirit reminded me this was a man in spiritual need, and I should talk to him.

But I wanted to be tactful, so I said, "Would you like to see our shipping room?"

"Yes," he said, "I would."

I had to hold his attention until an opportunity came for witness.

In the shipping room we talked about gummed tape, cardboard, wrapping paper, and then my eye fell on one of the tracts placed in outgoing packages.

"Every package leaving the plant contains one of these," I said, handing the leaflet to him.

He studied it a moment.

I prayed.

"This brings up a point," he said. "I've been looking for something in religion for two years. During the War I was stationed on Baker Island out in the Pacific, a mile and a half long and half a mile wide and not a tree on it. When we were off duty there was no place to go, so we talked. These guys were a bunch of intellectuals, skeptics you might say, and they explained away just about everything I ever believed in about God and the Bible.

"Two years ago my wife and I had a baby. When I looked at that baby, those beautiful hands and feet, everything so perfect, I knew there had to be miracles. That little body was a miracle, and right then I began believing in God again. But I've got a lot of questions on faith and the like that I'd like to get settled."

Now I understood why the Holy Spirit had urged me to give my witness to this man!

And perhaps you can understand why I say my office is my pulpit. This is as it should be, the crossing paths of life bringing us to people in spiritual need. And what better site than our own place of work, where the flow of conversation is more readily at our control?

I have learned to be alert for opportunities, to sense those whose hearts the Holy Spirit has prepared for further sowing of seed or, as is so often the case, for spiritual harvest.

Often unscheduled circumstances bring the most unique opportunities.

For example, I smashed my finger one morning when it caught between the belt and pulley of a metal-rolling mill in our plant. It was a double disappointment because an outstanding speaker was featured at a noon luncheon I wanted to attend. I hurried to the hospital, but they were busy in emergency that morning and delayed X-raying and patching up the mangled finger. I couldn't make it to the luncheon.

Disappointed and not hungry because of the pain I had suffered, I returned to the office. There stood a chap to whom I had witnessed many times but who repeatedly put me off with such statements as, "I've always been a good fellow. I go to church. I believe in Christ. I'll make it to heaven."

His life, however, was full of frustration, showing not a whit of evidence that he had ever been born again. At times he expressed spiritual concern, but when I tried to help him, he would go on the defensive.

But this morning was different. He had problems and was willing to talk about them.

"Why don't you take the first and most important step in solving problems?" I asked carefully, remembering the deft hands of the doctor at the hospital when he stitched my injured finger. "Until you know Christ, not just know about Him, you'll never have a real basis for finding answers in life."

"All right," he said without hesitation, "I'll do it."

Late that noon hour, when ordinarily I would have been listening to the last of a luncheon speaker's talk at a downtown hotel, this man opened his life to Jesus Christ.

You know, it wasn't until after two o'clock or so that I again noticed the throbbing pain in my finger!

Yes, opportunities are everywhere when people know you are Christ's representative.

I received a wonderful letter from Eastman Kodak Company expressing gratitude for the privilege of working with someone who put God first in his business. A similar letter came from one of the divisions of General Electric using our silver collectors. A Roman Catholic nun, who used a collector in the X-ray lab of the church hospital where she worked, wrote, "Mr. Tam, I don't use your silver collector for the money I get from the silver reclaimed. The only reason I use your silver collectors is that I know when I send in an old collector and ask for a new one, the package the new one comes in will have another of those wonderful gospel leaflets in it!"

A customer of ours in Stamford, Connecticut, went out of business and discontinued using the collectors, but about three months later he wrote and told me he now sold for a photographic supply house in New York City. He was a Jewish man with dynamic drive, and it was typical for him to say, "I don't see many of your silver collectors in the photo labs I visit. I liked them so well in my store back in Stamford I should be able to sell them like hot dogs at the ball park. How about letting me do it on commission?"

I set him up right away. He was a tremendous salesman and got us new accounts all over New England.

One day he wrote another letter saying, "You see how good I'm doing? Why don't you hire me full time? I like selling for you."

I wrote favorably concerning his suggestion but said I'd like to interview him first, so he promptly arranged to come to Lima.

He was a fireball of energy and initiative, and as we toured the plant and talked in my office, I saw what a fine salesman he would be on a full-time basis, so I hired him. I told him not only to keep going after new accounts but also to service older established users as well. He agreed.

Before long I got a letter in which he said, "Things are going great, but I've got one little problem. I go into one of your customer's labs and tell him I'm from States Smelting and Refining out there in Lima, and they look at me and say, 'Oh, you're from that religious company that has God for its partner,' and they want me to tell them about it. One fellow told me the men there had been discussing something from the Bible, and they naturally figured I'd have an answer for them, but all I can say when things like this come up is for them to write the question down, and I'll send it to you for an answer."

Three months later he wrote, "You know, Mr. Tam, I too am interested in your Jesus Christ."

On his next visit to the plant my wife and I invited him to our home for dinner. After the meal my wife wisely took the kiddies upstairs.

"Ed," I said, "that letter you wrote about being interested in my Jesus Christ really touched my heart. Actually, though, instead of you looking to me I really look to you. As a Jew, Ed, you are of the chosen race of God. We Christians love and respect you and your people for this, and we are sorry so many of your people are blind to the fact God sent Jesus, the Messiah, the Redeemer, through your race."

He listened wide-eyed as I took him first to the Old Testament, showing him how sin entered the human family through disobedience, how sacrificing was ordained, then into the New Testament showing how Christ came as an end to the Law and the old ways, giving us a new way through His life and death and resurrection.

That night, there in our living room, Ed knelt to acknowledge his Messiah as Redeemer and Lord. In the months ahead he gave vital evidence of genuine transformation.

Two years later as I sat at my desk, a long-distance call came from Stamford, Connecticut. I thought it was Ed calling in on a matter of business. It was his distraught wife telling me her husband had just died suddenly of a heart attack.

Tears came to my eyes. I couldn't restrain them. I didn't try. Not tears for Ed—because I knew he was with his Lord—but tears of gratitude for the Holy Spirit's firm but tender working in my life, teaching me obedience, disciplining me, guiding me.

I thought back to that Christmas in Rockford when God had spoken to me so clearly about the four thousand dollars underpaid to our customers. Ed's conversion dated back to that night. Had it not been for the refund checks and the opportunities they opened for my witness, the photofinishers would not have known about God being my senior partner and thus would not have stimulated Ed with Bible questions he couldn't answer.

17

Let me tell you about Joe Leatherman.

Joe was in his mid-thirties, sold for a food company, and was what the trade calls a real crackerjack. Because there was no relationship between his type of selling and our organization, the likelihood of his ever coming into our plant was nil.

But he came one day, came again and again, and here's the reason.

Joe did very well financially. He had a fine house outside the city, two automobiles, a speedboat. You name it. But it all added up to nothing, because in eight years of marriage, including the birth of two sweet little girls, he and his wife Eleanor could barely stand the sight of each other.

One morning, as they spewed at each other across the breakfast table, Eleanor screamed, "You want to know what I'd like to do? I'll tell you! I'd like to get a divorce!"

Her words hit Joe like a kick in the stomach.

For the first time in his life Joe prayed that morning. It went something like this: "Dear God, I'm in an awful mess here with my wife. I love her, and I want a happy home. Please help us get things straightened out. Please help us save our marriage."

A sense of relief came to his heart.

"As I look back," Joe says, "I can understand why I felt a bit of pressure roll off my back. That prayer didn't solve my problem, but it sort of turned the key to start the solution, because when a man asks God for help and when it isn't a selfish prayer but a real desire to know God and do what's right, God is sure to set some wheels in motion."

Joe is right.

God says, *You shall seek me and find me, when you shall search for me with your whole heart.*

Now, concerning Joe Leatherman, I want you to keep some important facts in mind. He came to us before we put up our stainless steel sign spelling out the words, CHRIST IS THE ANSWER. He didn't know me. There was no human explanation to his becoming interested in our plant. Call it coincidence if you must, but in my eyes the Joe Leatherman story documents the touch of miracle in personal evangelism, a case in which the Holy Spirit led directly to my desk a man seeking to know Christ.

Here's how it happened.

As a salesman Joe reported periodically to an office in Lima, usually coming in on Elida Road, which is U. S. 30. He had noticed construction work on our new plant, but it was of no significance to him. Our STATES SMELTING AND UNITED STATES PLASTIC CORP. lettering was up, but, as I said, we had not yet installed the CHRIST IS THE ANSWER testimonial.

He didn't know me. He didn't know of my interest in helping men find Christ.

Yet he subsequently told me, "It's a funny thing. I tell you, it was God's doing sure as anything. I'm driving in on U. S. 30 the morning I prayed asking the Lord to help me save my marriage. I come past your plant same as I'd done many times. I see this STATES SMELTING AND UNITED STATES PLASTIC sign. Then all of a sudden it seems like a voice is telling me I should go in and unload my problems to the guy who runs the place. Crazy, huh? I tell you, it made me feel kind of crazy. Well, I wasn't about to make a fool out of myself, so I drove by. I mean, how ridiculous could you get—walk into a strange place, ask for a strange man, tell him you and your wife are having a rough time of it?"

Joe decided to forget all about the impulse. Or so he thought!

But things got no better at home. On the impetus of his lone prayer that one morning Joe tried to ride with the crest, tried to ease the situation with his wife, but about the time she became more reasonable he would lose his temper, flare at her, and the mad merry-go-round was spinning full speed again.

"I drove past Mr. Tam's place again and again," Joe tells, "and every time I felt that urge, heard that inner voice. But I couldn't bring myself to do it."

One morning as Joe dressed to report to the office in Lima, a voice seemed to say, "You'll drive by that place again. Are you going to do as I have directed you?"

It seemed ridiculous.

Joe figured that if he did stop at our plant, someone would think he had mental problems and call the police.

"Shall I smite you?" a voice seemed to whisper in Joe's thoughts.

At that moment it occurred to him for the first time that this just might be God talking to him. He had prayed. He had asked God for help. Could this possibly be the way God would answer?

So coming in on Route 30 an hour or so later, Joe slowed down, flicked his blinker for a left turn.

But then he ran out of courage.

Turning off the blinker, he accelerated. Only for half a block, however. He had to go back. He didn't know why. He just knew he had to.

When the traffic cleared for a moment, he did a U-turn and drove back toward our plant.

Once again, however, he lost courage and drove on.

But once more he did a U-turn, came back, lost courage, drove, stopped again, turned back.

Finally he drove up to our visitor's parking area and came into the office.

"May I help you?" our receptionist asked.

"You sure can," Joe told her. "I want to speak with Mr. States."

"Mr. States?" The girl was taken off-guard a moment.

"The man who owns this place," Joe explained. "Isn't that his name out there on the front?"

"You mean Mr. Tam," the girl said.

She directed him to my office.

After introducing himself, telling me he sold for a large food wholesaler in town, Joe said, "I know you're not in the market for catsup. I'm not here to sell you anything."

I smiled.

"What can I do for you?" I asked.

"Well," Joe hedged a bit, "maybe you'll laugh at me, but I feel God told me to come in here."

I didn't laugh.

"You know anything about our business?" I asked.

"No, sir, I don't."

"I've spoken to several service clubs in the area and in a lot of churches. Have you ever been to a meeting where I was the speaker?"

He shook his head.

"Then did somebody tell you about me?"

No one had.

The reason Joe Leatherman came into my office was because a strong compulsion had come over him. It was the most unprecedented occurrence in all my efforts at personal evangelism.

"I tried hard enough to avoid coming," he said, "but I knew I had to, so today I did it."

"Tell me why you came," I said.

"I've got a problem."

"What's your problem?"

"Well, I live out there in that new housing area just west of town, and my wife and I have a beautiful place, a couple of nice little girls, but we're in deep trouble."

"In what way?"

"We're about to get divorced, and it tears me all up to think about it. I love my wife and our two kids, and I want to hold the home together, but I can't seem to make any headway. I prayed a while back, prayed to God, and as a result, or as near as I can figure, He keeps telling me to come see you."

I took out my Bible and opened it.

"What I need," Joe continued, "is advice on how to get along with my wife."

"No, Joe," I countered, "that isn't what you need."

"It sure is!"

"You need to learn how to get along with Jesus Christ."

Joe braced himself. I knew I had to be careful. He had his mind set on squaring things away with his wife, then going on living the way he had always done.

"Ever read the Bible?" I asked.

"To be real honest," Joe replied, "I've probably not read more than a page of it in my whole lifetime."

So I tried to show him God's plan of salvation, but he seemed confused. He told me later that he thought I was trying to induct him into some kind of secret society or an organization in which you learn a set of rules in order to qualify for membership.

I knew these were precarious moments. I could send him from my office and never see him again. It frightened me, the thought of letting him slip off the hook, and yet I saw we were making no progress.

"Why don't you take a few days to think about what we've talked about?" I suggested. "Then give me a call, and we'll get together and talk some more."

He left.

I bowed my head and prayed for this young man. I thanked God for sending him to me. I prayed he would come back, see his real need, and let the Holy Spirit show him the answer to that need.

He called several days later. He wanted to talk. I had the early part of the afternoon open and suggested we meet at one o'clock.

He arrived and there was a complete change in his attitude.

"I'd like to talk with you some more about this plan you tried to tell me about," he introduced.

"God's plan of salvation?"

"That's it."

Joe Leatherman became a new man that day!

Probably due to the uniqueness of our getting together in the first place, I took a special interest in Joe. He was very teachable, warm, and open-hearted. Joe became a kind of spiritual Timothy to me. We went together to speaking engagements, and I would have him give a brief testimony. One day as we stopped at a filling station I pushed him from the nest and told him to witness to the attendant. He did, and together we had the privilege of leading the man to Christ.

Eleanor, Joe's wife, did not respond quite so quickly. She questioned her husband's claims at first, wondering if religion might be his last-ditch stand to keep her from leaving. But as the months went by, she saw the change in his life, freedom from old habits, a new love and understanding toward her and the children.

She too invited the Son of God into her life.

I could go on at great length about Joe and Eleanor, our fellowship together, their growth as Christians. Joe continues selling, but for Moody Press, one of America's leading publishers of Christian literature. The two girls, older now of course, have followed their parents' spiritual example.

18

Once in a while I meet people who feel sorry for me because I have so little time for extracurricular activities. If the full life for the human male stems only from being an avid golfer, becoming an expert on the skeet range, hauling in sailfish off the Florida coast, or stunning the ladies with one's prowess at canasta, then life's best has passed me by. I haven't set out to be a social dude, but I do enjoy people, particularly those who have something to say. I like to relax.

But what in all the world enriches life more than to help others? And in a world where so many are confused and frustrated what can take precedence over the exciting exploit of helping a misguided man or woman find the Way?

I have only pity for Christians who have not allowed the Holy Spirit to lead them into the joy of harvest. Some plant the seed in witness. Some water the seed through counsel and example. Some gather the ripened grain in the decisive act of soul-winning. Each is strategic in the total reason for Calvary and the empty tomb. God never intended the thrill of evangelism to be the exclusive experience of a privileged few. It is for all Christians to enjoy if they will put first things first, if they will search the Scriptures and permit the Word of a God who lives to come alive in their personalities.

This is the utmost life.

I won't settle for anything less!

Why should anyone?

So, in this sharing my experiences in bringing men to Christ, please understand my purpose. It is not to put myself on display but to entice you to think of the potentials latent in your own life.

For once you have tasted the enriching manna, you too will be hard-pressed to find time for those temporal wheel-spinnings which promise release from boredom to so many people but which never quite live up to the adjectives on the label.

Soul-winning is the art of selling, raised to divine dimensions. A good salesman is always in demand. Many of them make more money than the men who supervise them. When a man sells successfully, he catches fire. You can't stop him. He goes from early morning till late at night. Selling. Selling. Selling.

Why, then, should it seem so odd for a man to be excited about telling lost men they can find redemption in Jesus Christ? If someone came up with the ultimate panacea for all human ills, it still would fall far short in significance to being able to tell a man he can have his sins forgiven, his character restored, his life made meaningful, and his eternal future secure.

Soul-winning is sheer adventure. No two experiences are ever the same. It's like being engulfed in the greatest of all drama. Take, for example, the time a Kiwanis club in our state invited me to speak at their luncheon on the topic of how God became my senior partner.

The editor of the local newspaper attended and was so impressed by what God had done for me that he ran excerpts of my testimony as a church page feature. As a result, I received a letter from an attorney in New Castle, Pennsylvania, a former resident of the town where I had spoken.

"Send me details on the legal procedure you went through to make God your senior partner," he wrote. "I'm very interested in this as an attorney."

I sent him the information, also including the plan of salvation.

Upon reading my letter, he telephoned.

"I've got to see you at once," he said. "Could I come to your office tomorrow afternoon?"

"Of course," I told him. "I'll be looking for you."

It was a drive of over two hundred miles.

"You may be just the person I've been looking for," he began, moments after entering my office. "I need spiritual help."

"I'll assist any way I can," I assured him.

"I attended law school at the University of Michigan," he continued. "When I graduated, ready for my career, I thought I would have a sense of satisfaction, but I didn't. It was quite the contrary. I knew I needed spiritual guidance, so I sought out a clergyman in Ann Arbor and told him my problem. He was very kind. I have no doubt that he tried to be helpful. But the best he seemed able to do was recite a few platitudes. I didn't find the peace I wanted in my heart.

"Then I moved to Canton, Ohio, where I had taken a position in a law office. I was busy learning the ropes, but my spiritual need hung over me like a sword on a thread. So I looked for a church in Canton. Here, again, the pastor was very kind. In fact, he was a wonderful fellow. I attended the church regularly. But nothing seemed to add up.

"I had a chance to better myself by moving to New Castle. First thing I looked for was a church. By this time I was feeling rather desperate. You know, in the law business you see people on their most sordid side, and this surely didn't help any.

"Well, it was a repeat performance at the third church. Then I read your story in our hometown newspaper which I take just to keep in touch, and I said to myself, this is what's wrong with me. I don't give enough money to the church. I figured if I'd do the way this fellow in Lima does, I might at least begin to find some meaning in life. That's why I wrote to you. But frankly, you confused me with that Bible verse from Ephesians. How does it go?"

"For by grace are you saved through faith: and that not of yourselves; it is the gift of God: not of works, lest any man should boast," I quoted.

"Could you explain that to me?"

That afternoon this Pennsylvania attorney knelt in my office and received the grace of God through faith in Jesus Christ. Peace came at last to his heart. We've kept in touch, and it's thrilling to learn of the many ways God is now using him as a Christian attorney to bring peace to others.

Hungry hearts are everywhere. They don't want religion; they want a living experience. Only Christ can give this.

Now, it is my last intention to criticize the organized Church. I've been an active churchman for years and expect to remain one until I die. But too often people think of church as a relationship apart from life. It's something you do on Sunday, but it scarcely relates to what you do the remainder of the week. This is why lay witness is so important. You and I touch men in the crossroads. We see them as they are, and they see us as we are, sleeves rolled up, hard at it, no pretense. No Sunday front. And this is where the gospel is most relevant.

The hardest thing I ever did, and it was only by God's help, was to overcome shyness in talking to others about my faith. People talk of religion as a private matter. Well, maybe religion is and should be, but a living faith is something different. If I saw a man dying of suffocation, I'd try to get air to him. People are dying of spiritual suffocation today. They need the energizing breath of faith.

But I still subscribe to the premise that we ought not to force our faith on anyone. I would never intentionally pressure a person to become a believer or even to listen to my witness. This is the place of the Holy Spirit in our lives. The Bible says, *One plants, another waters, but God gives the increase.* As you travel, as you rub elbows with people in the workaday world, as you make contacts through your church, you will find people whom the Holy Spirit has prepared for your witness. They won't be offended at your testimony. They will welcome it. In fact, you would do them a wrong not to witness to them.

Let me give you a specific example.

En route to speak at a college function in New York, I sat beside a man on the plane who wore a religious pin. This, of course, provided a natural entreé for conversation. We talked for several moments. I discovered he had a very active church life. But there was an absence of real spiritual content to what he told me. He said a lot about the Church, nothing about Christ.

So I asked him, "Have you ever thought of becoming a Christian?"

"Why," he said, recoiling just a bit, "I think I am a Christian."

"Would you tell me what it means to be one?" I asked.

"Well," he began, "a Christian is . . . uh . . . ."

He cleared his throat.

I smiled, trying to put him at ease.

"I, uh," he resumed, "I think a Christian is . . . he's . . . a . . . uh. . . ."

Again he stopped. A look of blank frustration came to his face.

"To be real honest," he said meekly, "I guess I don't know for sure what a Christian is."

"Would you care to discuss it further?"

"I surely would."

So we did.

He had a tender heart that day. He had just come from Minneapolis where he had attended the funeral of a close relative and had been doing much thinking, about life, about death.

There on the plane that day he bowed his head and invited Christ into his heart.

One of my earlier opportunities for witnessing in flight came on a plane from Latin America. It was a tourist flight, and we were packed in like sardines. At San Juan I had stood in line to clear customs, and just ahead of me was an army man. We struck up a casual conversation, then separated as we boarded the plane.

Shortly after takeoff, however, the Holy Spirit began to speak to me about that man, and I had a strong compulsion that if I didn't talk to him about his spiritual condition, no one ever would.

"But, Lord," I reasoned, "this is a crowded airplane. This is no place to do witnessing. I'd embarrass the man."

Yet the compulsion grew stronger.

"All right," I prayed, "if You will make it possible, I'll witness."

The prayer had scarcely been uttered when the man squeezed his way out of the seat and walked to the front. I stood and followed him. There was a map of the Carribean by the door, and the pilot periodically called out information.

"Where are we now?" I asked.

"I think about here," he said, pointing.

I prayed for guidance.

We looked another moment.

Then I whispered, "Pardon me, sir, but I've been praying for you."

He turned to me, surprised but not in the least displeased.

"Are you interested in spiritual things?"

"Yes, sir, I am!"

"Would you give me the privilege of talking to you?"

"I'd like that very much."

My wife was with me. She gave up her seat so the soldier and I could sit together.

"I have my Bible in my briefcase," I said. "Would it embarrass you if I took it out so we could look at it together?"

"Not at all," he assured me.

I have seldom seen a man more open, more willing. Nor can I ever forget his prayer that day as he thanked God for sending a Christian across his path and as he asked Christ to claim his life.

Remember the verse quoted earlier, *One plants, another waters, but God gives the increase?* Sometimes this will be the case with you. You will sow the seed, another will harvest the fruit. Right here, though, let me emphasize one point. Always try to bring people to a point of decision when you witness. Don't pressure, of course, but don't hedge, either. A salesman who presents his product, gets the customer all interested, but makes no effort to close the sale, is doomed to failure.

Having said this, though, let me again emphasize the fact that you may not always be the one who harvests. You may only be the one who sows.

For example, several years ago while walking in Chicago, I passed through a park area where some girls were playing softball. I became so interested watching them that I grew careless and walked right into a concrete lamppost, cutting myself above the eye.

I returned to the hotel, summoned the house physician, and he stitched the wound for me, asking me to come back the following Wednesday so he could check it.

He wasn't busy that afternoon and was in a mood to talk, so I knew I should introduce my witness. But I didn't.

It bothered me so much that I sent him a booklet by a Christian doctor, thinking this would be the end of the contact.

A year later while on a speaking engagement at a church in Niagara Falls, the Lord spoke to me with unmistakable clarity about my failure to utilize the opportunity of witnessing to the doctor in Chicago. The conviction became so intense that I finally promised God I would get in touch with the man as soon as I returned to Lima.

A wellspring of peace came to my heart as a result of that promise to God, and I'm convinced it was this prayer which caused my Niagara weekend to be so singularly blessed in the church meetings.

Back in Lima I called Chicago. The doctor remembered me, readily gave me an appointment, and next morning I once again headed west on Route 30.

His office was jammed, and it was well beyond the appointment hour before the nurse called me into one of the consultation rooms. After a few moments the doctor entered.

"Good afternoon, Mr. Tam," he greeted cordially. He had my file card in his hand. "How's the eye?"

"My eye is fine," I said.

He looked at me momentarily perplexed.

"Doctor," I said, "I suppose I'm the strangest patient you've ever had. I've come to Chicago to talk to you about your soul."

"Oh yes," he said, "I remember you. You sent me a booklet written by a doctor. I read it, and I'm interested. Do you have anything else I can read?"

"I haven't brought any reading material," I said, "and I realize this is a busy day for you."

"They're all busy," he commented, smiling.

"Well," I continued, "life gets a little busy for me at times, too. But I was in Niagara Falls over the weekend for a speaking engagement, and I became deeply persuaded I must come to Chicago and share my personal testimony with you."

"I'd like to hear it," he said.

He sat back casually. He didn't glance at his watch. For fifteen minutes he listened as I gave him a digested account of my experience.

Then he said, "Mr. Tam, as you know, I've got an office full of patients, and I can't take any more time, but let me thank you most sincerely for coming to my office and talking to me this way. I assure you I'll never forget it, and I'll give careful consideration to what you've said."

Though this concluded my contact with the doctor, I have assurance in my heart of meeting him in heaven someday!

One of the road signs to watch for in this adventure of witnessing is times of disappointment. *The steps of a righteous man are ordered of the Lord,* the Bible tells us, and so when problems come, it is often because, as someone has put it, "disappointment is really His appointment."

This has happened to me numerous times, such as the recent example of a flight to Montana where I had an appointment to speak in a town up near the Canadian border.

"Lord," I prayed, "help me witness to someone on the flights today."

I use the Dayton airport down Interstate 75, an hour's drive from my house, and as I boarded the plane that day I found it with only a light load. No one came to occupy the seat next to me.

Chicago to Minneapolis was the same as was the plane from Minneapolis to Billings.

It bothered me.

Out of Billings the travel agent had me booked on a trunk airline flight north, and so I went to the desk to check in.

"Sorry, sir," the agent said, "but that flight's cancelled for today."

"When's the next flight?" I asked.

"Not till seven tomorrow morning."

"But I've got to get there. I have a speaking engagement tonight."

"Sorry, sir."

I stepped away from the counter and silently thanked God for this disappointment, asking Him to show me the reason for it.

Just then another man stepped up to the counter, a big, burly character who, when he learned of the cancelled flight, let out with an air-blueing stream of profanity.

"Look," he bellowed, "you get me on a flight! I'm gonna lose a lotta money if I don't get up there!"

"I'm sorry," the agent said meekly. "There's nothing I can do."

A third man came to check in for the flight. He too displayed his temper, though not so vociferously as the first.

I stepped up to the two men. "Since there are three of us," I said, "why don't we charter a plane?"

"Good idea!" the big fellow exclaimed. Turning to the agent he said, "Get us some information right away on charter flights!"

In a few minutes we were out beside a small plane. The big fellow sat up front with the pilot, we two smaller men in the back.

"My name is Malcom Randall," my companion introduced himself.

"I'm Stanley Tam," I said. "What's your business?"

"I work for the government. You?"

"I'm from Lima, Ohio. We reclaim and refine silver and also have a plastics sales organization."

"You're here on business?"

"I'm speaking at a church tonight, telling about my experiences as a Christian businessman."

"That's fascinating. I wish I could hear you, but I'll be tied up with appointments."

"Would you let me share some of my experiences with you now?"

"Sure, why not?"

So I began my story.

"Say," he interrupted, "I've heard you speak! It was at a service club or something."

His sudden outburst threw me off for a moment.

"Well, how about that?" I said.

"Yeah, I sure have." He pointed to a pin on his lapel. "It was at a Lion's Club meeting somewhere. I'm out of town a lot, but I always try to get to the local club wherever I happen to be. Isn't that something?"

It so intrigued him to have run across me before, I had difficulty getting back on course.

But finally he said, "Go ahead. Finish the story."

As I continued, he grew more intensely attentive. I could see evidence of spiritual concern creep across his countenance.

"You know," he said when I had concluded my testimony, "almost every night I get down on my knees and try to pray. I confess my sins."

"Do you have God's peace in your heart?" I asked.

He shook his head. "That's something I know nothing about," he said.

"May I tell you how to find this peace?" I asked.

He nodded.

Moments later there on the plane God honored me with the privilege of bringing another man to a personal knowledge of His Son.

"You know something," this man said to me, "it was no accident the plane was cancelled out of Billings. It was an act of God. He knew I needed to meet you!"

Our plant was burglarized some years back. I complained about it to my wife. Didn't we put everything we had into God's care? Then why did this happen?

I soon understood.

An enterprising salesman in another city saw the story in the paper and came to sell me a burglarproof safe. For years this man had been seeking spiritual peace. The search ended there in my office.

I've said soul-winning gives drama to life, and it surely does. Perhaps the most outstanding example of this in my experience occurred the day an elderly man came to my office. The minute I saw him I recognized him, though I hadn't seen him in over thirty years. I told you earlier the beginning of this amazing drama. Now let me fill you in on the conclusion.

Holding up a slip of paper, the unexpected visitor said, "I got your name and address from a customer of mine. He said he's been converted, and I saw such a change in his life from what it had been before that I asked him to tell me about it. He told me you were the one who led him to faith, and when I told him this looked like what I needed, he gave me your name and address. I was wondering if you had time to talk to me."

"I surely have!" I exclaimed. "Sit down."

He sat. He seemed nervous, so I wondered if he recognized me. "Have we met before?" I asked.

"No sir," he said, "I don't believe we have, Mr. Tam. This customer of mine said you do a lot of speaking in service clubs and the like, but I've never had the privilege of hearing you."

It was an excruciating discipline to keep from saying what lurked on the tip of my tongue, but I managed to hold back. Instead I got down to life's most important business.

"I'm in pretty bad shape physically, as you can see," the man said. He leaned a pair of crutches against my desk. "I'll die soon, and I'm not ready for it."

"You can be," I told him. "The reason God sent His Son into the world was so you and I could have eternal life. This means death can become nothing more than an entry into more reality than we could ever know here on earth."

"How does a man obtain this eternal life?"

I told him.

"If I could believe that . . ." he said, his eyes moist.

"Either it's true or God is a liar," I said. "You don't believe God would lie to us do you?"

"Oh no, Mr. Tam, I sure don't believe that!"

"The reason God gave us the Bible," I continued, "is so we can know for sure how much He loves us and how He has provided for our eternal salvation." I got out my Bible and showed him the words of cleansing and assurance and peace. There at my desk he bowed to receive the gift of salvation.

I kept in close touch with him. He asked for no help, but when his health failed so he couldn't work, I gave him economic aid. I have never seen anyone more sincerely grateful.

"You sure are God's answer to my need," he told me.

"That's one of the blessings of life," I said, "helping one another."

"I sure wish I could have got to know you sooner."

I opened my mouth to speak but didn't.

The day came when I received a telephone call telling me this man had died. Tears came to my eyes as I thanked God for permitting me to bring the news of His grace to such a needy heart.

I guess they were tears of anticipation, too.

Anticipation for the day when we shall meet in heaven. Then I'm sure he will remember that the person who led him to Christ was also the one to whom he had thirty years earlier made a five-dollar down payment on a hard-earned Model T, inveigled possession of the title, then refused to pay the remainder of the debt!

Stanley Tam in his younger days, pouring molton silver from the tilting furnace into ingots.

When we built our present complex—5 acres under roof. I wanted to include a visual witness. "Christ is the Answer" has been a blessing to many.

Now that the children are grown and gone, I'm home less than before. But I do set aside time to be with my dear wife, Juanita.

19

I don't wonder at the upheavals we see in the world today—disrespect for law and order, the generation gap, tailoring ethics to fit a given situation, rejection of such absolutes as the Ten Commandments, erudite men seriously considering the demise of God.

God can become authentic to a society, and the precepts of the Bible can only be validated, only when ordinary people like you and me permit the Holy Spirit to make us living examples of spiritual reality.

But how often do we see someone who evidences concern to be a testimonial of the reality of God?

Yet, in my travels through the years, meeting many different kinds of people, I sense a common hunger in just about everyone's heart. We want to help others. We want meaningful lives. Even in the worst of men a spark of good glows; some call it the spark of divine life, but nowhere does the Bible substantiate this, so I call it the yearning of a lost soul for redemption.

In the recounting of these numerous episodes in my life you have seen the route one must take to assure personal redemption.

But, as the birth of a child is but the beginning of physical life, so also the moment of conversion is but the start of spiritual life. Prayer, study of the Bible, application of the truths of the Bible to the warp and woof of Monday through Saturday—these are the growth factors in the Christian life. Yet undergirding all this is the word with which I introduced my testimony.

Obedience.

Jesus says, *"You must be born again."*

When a man obeys this injunction, he is converted; he becomes a new creation in Christ.

Present your bodies a living sacrifice, the Bible tell us. *Be not conformed to this world, but be transformed.*

When a man obeys this precept, he walks the road to true discipleship.

In our feverish world today we often hear people quote the famous prayer of St. Francis. It is a beautiful prayer. In it he says: "Lord, make me an instrument of Thy peace. . . . It is in giving that we receive. . . . It is in dying that we are born to eternal life."

Beautiful words.

Meaningful.

But they are mere platitudes until we isolate that one word, "instrument," and recognize the impossibility of becoming a tool in God's hands unless we first submit ourselves without reservation to His control.

How might this happen to you?

Let's presume you are a beginner in the Christian life. You try to read the Bible, and it's like a textbook—written in your language but almost completely outside your frame of reference. You don't understand how a very real entity such as yourself can converse with an unseen, humanly unprovable Presence. The thought of ever engaging in the most constructive of all benevolences—that of helping lost souls find faith—terrifies you.

Yet, something stirs in your heart. Take away the bricks and mortar, the bank account and the credit standing, and your life doesn't add up to much.

But you want it to.

Well, right there is the beginning: wanting to escape the mediocrity of yourself and to come into a reality beyond yourself.

This reality is God.

You identify with this reality by being sure of your personal salvation, then by obedience to the directives God gives His children in His Word.

It is as simple . . . and as profound . . . as that!

Try to remember one concept as you search for meaning in your life through obedience to God. The Bible is a very conclusive book. Scholars have devoted lifetimes to its study and lamented their ability to no more than scratch the surface of its awesome contents. Yet—and this is the majesty of the Bible—God's message to man is best characterized by its simplicity. It was written to little children, to those stumbling in the search for faith, and God never intended it to confuse you.

While I respect the sincere theologian and in no way question his skill or integrity, I sometimes wonder if the problems some people have in understanding the Bible are because they fail to approach it in childlike, humble, and contrite anticipation.

Thy word is a lamp unto my feet and a light unto my path, the Psalmist wrote, which is exactly as God intended it to be.

Now perhaps you expect me to give you some secret formula for making the Bible come alive in your experience. If so, I must disappoint you. The Bible is an intensely personal book. God prepared it as a personal message to every human being on earth.

How tragic to think of the millions who miss this awesome privilege!

I cannot give you a secret formula, because no such formula exists. Each individual discovers the Bible for himself.

I can only once again insist that the discovery must have obedience as its foundation. God tells you to have a clean heart and mind, and you obey Him. He tells you to let love become basic to all you are and do, and you obey Him. He tells you to exercise concern for the souls of others, and you obey Him. You let Him relate these commands to you personally, to your authentic self as He designed you, your characteristics, your talents, your personality.

And when you do, this obedience opens the door to a horizonless continuity of blessing.

I do not know of a marriage that has ended in the divorce courts when both the husband and wife were true believers in the Lord Jesus Christ and sincerely endeavored to obey God in their lives. I do not know of an instance where children from such a home ever appeared in juvenile court. I do not know of such an individual who cheated in his job, or who broke the laws of his community, or who came to the end of his years in disillusionment.

Life is meant to be full and rich and wonderful for the Christian. I know, for I have found it abundantly so!

As I say, it is a continuity of blessing.

First, blessing comes to your personal life. God is in the business of changing people. His masterpiece is not Adromeda thrust two and a half billion light years into outer space. His masterpiece is you, conformed daily toward the image of Christ through the Holy Spirit's molding of your life as you search and find and obey the concepts and precepts of the Bible.

You can and should be a better person today than you were yesterday. The Bible is both prognosis and therapy, a mirror and a window. *Grow in grace and in the knowledge of our Lord and Savior Jesus Christ,* the Bible entreats. I make a point of frequently taking inventory of my life. What are the rough edges needing to be made smooth? What are the strengths of character on which I can build by God's help?

As transformation comes to your personal life, so also will come enrichment to your intimate associations.

Juanita and I are two quite ordinary people. We have our blind spots, our imperfections, but we have sincerely endeavored to put Christ at the center of our marriage and at the head of our home. The result has been the retention of the romance which characterizes two people genuinely falling in love, and the maturity of relationship which alone can keep a marriage fresh and meaningful and enriching. Each of us has those personal liabilities which could have spoiled our marriage, but they have been subordinated to the vanishing point because of the presence of Christ in our lives.

Really now, how many attainments are there in life which take precedent over the building of an endearing marriage and a happy home? Both are for the asking when Christ is put first in each relationship.

It has been several years now since we turned over one hundred percent of our business to the Lord. Have we been sorry for this? Would we have done differently if we had the choice again?

To answer those questions, let me share some thoughts which came to me during a time of recent meditation.

There is a particularly practical rendition of Matthew 6:19-21 in *The Bible in Basic English,* in which Jesus said: *"Make no store of wealth for yourselves on earth, where it may be turned to dust by worms and weather, and where thieves may come in by force and take it away. For where your wealth is, there will your heart be."*

In this translation there are only sixty-eight words, and it is not in any sense a treatise; it is only a hint for wise men. It is a vital and practical truth which the foolish will continue to ignore but to which the wise will take good heed. It is supported by the entire New Testament and represents a highly condensed summary of the teaching of our Lord Jesus Christ and the apostles on the matter of earthly wealth.

Christ is here teaching a most wonderful possibility—that of the transmutation of our earthly wealth into a store of higher and eternal values which will abide forever. I take that word "transmutation" from the old medieval concept that someday the alchemists would come up with a formula for changing a base metal such as common lead into a precious metal such as gold. This is what "transmutation" means—the changing across to something else.

What a staggering concept!

Here I am in my fifties, looking back across years which have sped by at incredible speed. I hope to have many more productive years, but at best my life is more than half over. Suppose Juanita and I had kept the stock? We would have more than a quarter of a million dollars in profits each year after taxes. For what?

A home in Florida? Investments? A beautiful mausoleum in which to be interred one day?

A man can eat only one meal at a time, wear only one suit of clothes at a time, drive only one car at a time. All this I have. Isn't it enough?

It is, and I have no desire for more. Instead, we have "sent it on ahead," as someone once put it. We live comfortably and extremely happily. We have all we need. And we're transmuting the efforts of this life into eternal stocks and bonds.

But transmutation is more than material. A Christian's efforts in soul-winning, standing by his pastor and church, sharing with other Christians in the cause of Christ—all of this is also investment for eternity.

In this vein, let me share one of the special joys in my life.

While visiting my office one day, a leader in a prominent Christian organization told me of a movement among Christian businessmen in several areas of the country. The idea is to select a prayer partner, another man with whom you meet once a week to share in confidence problems and challenges in a spirit of prayer.

It sounded great, so I decided to give the idea a try.

My partner's name is Art. He owns a medical supply house. We meet in the city park.

First, we chitchat about business, then share evidences of God's blessing. He has five salesmen on the road and keeps me informed of their progress. I confide information on our two corporations. We are like unofficial partners in each other's business. We talk about our families. We share insights from the Bible. We pray.

It's an enriching arrangement. It attests to the promises God has made in His Word to hear and answer prayer.

Art's son fell in love with a girl in college, a fine girl, but one who could not tolerate the evangelical faith.

We gave much time to discussing and praying about the matter.

"I told him I wouldn't finance his college," Art said one day, "but now his girl friend's father tells him he'll do it instead."

They set a wedding date. Art and I continued praying.

Just before they announced nuptials, with no impetus from Art except his prayers, the two broke up.

Often we pray for those to whom one of us is witnessing, and we have seen remarkable answers.

Pete Peterson is the most outstanding example.

His wife had come to our church for some ten years, but her husband was cold as stone to the Christian message. Art and I decided to make it a matter of intense prayer concern.

Then all of a sudden Pete sold his house and moved to California, where he purchased a gasoline service station.

It was discouraging at first, but we kept praying for another three months. Then I received a speaking invitation for a retreat in California and, checking the map, discovered the campgrounds were only seven miles from Pete's town!

"I'll keep praying while you're out there," Art promised.

First chance I had, I got in touch with Pete. He was surprisingly open and friendly. I found it easy to talk to him.

"Pete," I said as we got down to the point, "you've run as far as you can from God. Today is the day for you to make a decision to receive Christ as your Savior."

Pete looked squarely at me, his eyes glistening.

"You're right," he said.

We knelt there in his home as Peter Peterson became a new creature in Christ. That night he came to the retreat where I was speaking and gave a wonderful witness. His wife told us later how rapidly he grew in the Christian life.

Art and I spent a good while thanking God for the answer to our prayers.

But the greatest impetus for gratitude came three weeks after my return when I received a telephone call from Mrs. Peterson.

"Pete's dead," she sobbed. "There was a holdup at his service station, and the bandit shot him through the head. Oh, I'm so thankful you helped him come to Christ before he died! He was so happy in his new Christian faith!"

Another result of my intercession fellowship with Art has been the establishment of a Christian radio station in our town. But that's a story in itself.

Our fellowship has given me a continually enlarging concern for people in my own community. Sometimes it's a lot easier to talk about one's faith among strangers than to your own neighbors.

We have started a Bible class in our plant. It meets every Thursday night. We try to make it a complement to local churches rather than in any way competitive. It was begun first of all to help new converts in and around Lima but has since become a spiritual rescue station on its own.

Normal attendance is eighteen to twenty-five, but sometimes it swells to over forty. In all, about a hundred people are involved.

One night a woman and her daughter came from a small town outside Lima.

"Do you allow Roman Catholics in your Bible class?" she asked.

"Of course," I assured her. "Several Catholics attend these sessions. There are some here tonight."

"I'm a Catholic," she said. "I've heard about the Bible studies for two years. Many times I've driven past this building on Thursday nights, but not until tonight did I have the courage to come in and see what a Protestant meeting is like."

She came regularly for six months. Then one night she told us she was ready to open her heart to Christ.

Soon her husband began coming, and the night came when he too became a new person.

The daughter who came that first night with the mother was in nurse's training in Lima but attended as often as she could. On one of those nights she stood near the pop cooler. Wishing to be cordial, I asked if she would like a bottle.

"No, thank you," she said. "I came for only one reason tonight. I too want to give my heart to Christ."

In four years we have seen over one hundred people converted, and the number keeps growing.

Where outside the Christian life can one find adventures more exciting and rewarding? When people speak of Christianity as a dull and antiquated experience, pity wells in my heart. God created us with but one objective in mind—to equip us to become His children through faith in His Son and obedience to His Word.

And only in this faith does life add up to peace and fulfillment.

People ask me about my plans for the future. Since I have no sons, what will happen to the business? I'm concerned about this and am seeking God's guidance, but I'm far more anxious to be sure I am in the center of His will for my life today.

He has a plan for my life. He has a plan for yours. He has led me in one way. He may lead you in another.

It is through obedience that we fit into this plan.

Obedience.

I have never been able to look back upon a year and feel it has been lived in complete obedience to my Lord's commands. I'm too human. But I do thank Him for what He has done in my life as a result of obedience, and I look forward to tomorrow in anticipation.

God owns my business, and God owns me.

I have every confidence He will take good care of His property!

20

And Then Another Decade

During the six years following publication of this book, a lot of good things happened. My country celebrated her bicentennial. The business continued to boom. Juanita and I built a new house, shared in the responsibilities for a new church. A half-dozen grand children were born. We made several overseas trips.

But I also heard our doctor and a consulting specialist say, "Stanley, you have at most two years to live."

Details appear in a new book Ken Anderson and I have prepared, a compilation of adventures my Lord has permitted me to have in the world's most important enterprise— helping men and women discover a living and eternal faith.

As the years passed, we outgrew our previous facilities and purchased thirty-three acres along I-75, erected buildings occupying five acres of floor space, and expanded from our four million dollars a year to thirteen—heading toward my goal of twenty.

In my new film, *The Answer,* actor Harry Elders depicts the tense staff meeting when, during the bottoming out of a business slump, I again emphasized that our business is not controlled by the economy but by God.

Reading my Bible one morning, God made personal to me the verse in the eighth chapter of Deuteronomy, which reads:

Remember the Lord your God, for it is He who gives you the ability to produce wealth.

It was as though that promise had been written just for me!

We are presently able to provide three million dollars each year for missionary outreach across the world. Investing this money through Every Creature Crusade, which involves nearly one hundred teams in a dozen different countries, we see between forty and fifty indigenous churches established every month.

To me, making money becomes pointless unless one's objective is to help others.

We have America's largest inventory of industrial plastic items. Our catalog sits on the purchasing officer's desk in just about every major corporation, plus thousands of smaller enterprises. We want sales volume, of course, but only if we can provide quality and top service at fair prices. To do otherwise is to cheat oneself, for the mere accumulation of wealth can impoverish a man.

I like to make money. It's big adventure, sending out the catalog—our only paid means of advertising—and seeing orders come in. At five o'clock every night, our loading dock is a hive of activity. My son-in-law, Wes Lytle, and I watch our growth charts with mutual delight.

But to me, without question, the biggest business in the world, and life's greatest and most rewarding adventure, is to help people discover—as my family and so many people in our company have discovered—what it means to have a valid relationship with God through His Son, Jesus Christ.

The inside cover of our catalog, where we tell customers about our faith, together with the literature we enclose with every order, causes over seven hundred people each year to write and tell us they, too, have put their trust in our Savior.

This book you are reading has become a silent evangelist, and no month passes without my receiving several telephone calls . . . or having business people come to my office . . . as readers indicate their desire to know our wonderful Lord.

In conjunction with the initial publication of this book, we produced a motion picture by the same title, *God Owns My Business.* We make this available to business and industrial groups without charge, and many have been born again as a result.

More recently, we produced *The Answer,* a motion picture which updates our story and tells about the miraculous way—alone in my hospital room—I was delivered from the death sentence of cancer.

Both of these films can be obtained in DVD format. Just write or call our company.

United States Plastic Corp.
1390 Neubrecht Road
Lima, OH 45801
Or call (419) 228-2242 or FAX (419) 228-5034

The role of books, films and the witness of our business was poignantly illustrated recently when I attended a mail order catalog seminar in Chicago.

Initially, when those attending saw our catalog with its inside cover, I fell prey to broadsides of censure.

Ken and I relate the story more fully in the other book.

Let me just tell you here that, without my making a comment, seminar participants themselves rose to my defense, and one of the men—to whom I gave a copy of this book—took the book home and put it in a dresser drawer.

Months later, returning from work, he turned on television, saw the last half of our first film, recognized the story as relating to the Chicago catalog seminar. He remembered where he put the book, read it, and then called to tell me he had become a transformed man through placing his faith in the Lord Jesus.

That's where real wealth lies!

As long as God gives me the strength, and as I carefully turn command of the business over to my son-in-law, I want to devote my energy and ideas and initiative to the prime objective of learning more and more about putting one's life and endeavors under the control of our Heavenly Father.

Why don't you do the same?

If I can help, please let me hear from you!

Stanley Tam
United States Plastics Corp.
1390 Neubrecht Road
Lima, Ohio 45801

21

22 Secrets of Success
That You Can Use in Your Life
How to Eliminate Problems in Your Christian Life

1. **Make a Commitment**—This is the first step to produce fruit.

   - Make a spiritual altar and completely surrender yourself to God—your eyes, ears, mouth, mind, hands, feet, and your goals in life. Ask the Holy Spirit to make you a minister in the marketplace. *You did not choose me, but I chose you and appointed you to go and bear fruit—fruit that will last. Then the Father will give you whatever you ask in my name* (John 15:16).

   - On this same spiritual altar, place your home and ask the Holy Spirit to make it a ministry for the Lord's work.

   - On this same spiritual altar, place your business—*But seek first his kingdom and his righteousness, and all these things will be given to you as well* (Matthew 6:33).

Ask Him to make your business a pulpit from which to minister.

- Mrs. Long's ministry in soul winning. (See Chapter 3, pages 12-14.)

- Be honest in the little things, like pens and pencils that don't belong to you.

- *Remain in me, and I will remain in you. No branch can bear fruit by itself; it must remain in the vine. Neither can you bear fruit unless you remain in me* (John 15:4). Read this again. You must believe this. **STOP**—Do this now!

2. **Obey**—Samuel said, *Does the Lord delight in burnt offerings and sacrifices as much as in obeying the voice of the Lord? To obey is better than sacrifice, and to heed is better than the fat of rams* (1 Samuel 15:22). When God talks to you, take action. Too many times we put it off and forget, and then we say, "Why doesn't God use me?" You can have anything in your Christian life through obedience. Believe this.

- Whom do you promote in your personal life? In your career? You are a pulpit. Use your business to preach the Gospel.

- **$4,000 Refund**

  One year, as we were closing our books, my accountant came to me and said that we had sold more silver than we had purchased from our customers. What we had done was run the assays too low. If the silver was ninety-five percent pure, we had called it ninety-four percent. I didn't give it much thought. I was in a hurry to leave the business and get to Rockford, IL, to my in-laws' home for Christmas.

  One evening everyone wanted to go to bed early. I told my wife that I was going to stay up and pray. As I was praying, I said, "Lord, this is the end of the year. Is there anything in my life that shouldn't be there?

At once the Lord replied, "Yes, there is. You have $4,000 that doesn't belong to you."

I replied, "Lord, we have 3,000 customers and $4,000. I think that is coming out at the end of the year pretty close."

The Lord replied, "But you have $4,000 that doesn't belong to you."

I answered, "That might be true, but our customers would all get something different. It wouldn't be worth all the work it would take to figure what each one would receive."

I had learned this before. When I disobeyed the Lord, He pulled the switch. The power in my life went off. I didn't want that to happen again. I said, "Lord, I will make that refund."

We hired a lady who worked on this project for six weeks. We had 3,000 refunds to mail. The lowest was $.07 in stamps, and the highest was $17.

Just as we were ready to mail the refunds, the Lord said, "I want you to tell them why they are getting this refund." We typed a letter to our customers explaining that we deeded more than fifty-one percent of the business to the Lord, that He told us we had a $4,000 overrun and that we should refund our customers. We mailed this letter with the refunds.

I told the ladies in the office, "We won't hear from our customers now because we put that spiritual letter in with the refunds. They will be too embarrassed to write us and thank us."

We were not prepared to receive hundreds of letters. One was from Eastman Kodak Co., saying how they appreciated us—a company who would make a small refund. A Catholic hospital in Indiana wrote that they didn't use our silver collectors for the money they received, but because they look forward to the Gospel tract they found in each replacement silver collector.

It is currently 2011; we have been placing a Gospel tract in each shipment for 70 years. This year we are making 300,000 shipments. Each month we receive approximately 25 replies from customers, indicating they have made a decision for Christ. We write a personal letter to each one, send them a copy of our book and enroll them in the Navigators follow-up courses.

I went to our local camera shop to purchase film. The owner came out with a check and said he wanted to return it to me. I said, "No," and told him what we had done. He said that salesmen coming from all over the country ask him what kind of company we have here in Lima that we made a refund to the industry. It was great advertising! We got our $4,000 back in only three months in new business!

I had a customer in New York City who went out of business. (See also Chapter 16, pages 128-130.) He started selling photographic supplies in New England. One day he wrote me a letter, saying, "I used to use your silver collectors, and I made some money from them. But I didn't see many of them here in New England. Why don't you let me sell them here on commission?" If he didn't sell any of them, it didn't cost me anything.

One day he wrote another letter and said, "See how many silver collectors I have sold for you? Why don't you hire me full time?" I wrote back and requested that he come to the factory. I sized him up and thought that he would be an asset, so I hired him.

He began to write more letters. "I called on a customer, and he said, 'You are from that religious company out in Ohio. We had a discussion here the other day, and somebody asked a religious question. Nobody could answer it.' They turned to me and asked me the question. I told them that it was out of my department, but I will send it to my boss, and he will answer it for you. You know, Mr. Tam, since I have taken this job, I have gotten into many religious discussions which, frankly, I know nothing about. I am interested in knowing more about what the company believes."

The next time he came to the plant, I invited him to my home for dinner. After the meal my wife, wise in soul winning, took the children upstairs so that we could be alone. After many Scripture verses and questions and answers, my friend got down on his knees and accepted Christ as his Savior.

Years went by when one day I received a phone call in my office from his wife, saying, "Ed is dead. He had a heart attack in one of the office buildings in New York City and died."

As I replaced the phone, my thoughts were, "What if I had not made that refund to our customers? Ed wouldn't have received his refund. He wouldn't have called me. We wouldn't have met. He would have gone to hell." To obey is better than sacrifice.

3. **Bind the Devil** — *I tell you the truth, whatever you bind on earth will be bound in heaven, and whatever you loose on earth will be loosed in heaven* (Matthew 18:18). People complain about all kinds of problems in their lives and blame someone else for them. It isn't your boss or friend or wife or husband; you are looking in the wrong place. It is the Devil. We have only one enemy. Bind him and stop all the problems at their source.

- Youth Camp, Merel Fuller, Director
- **Binding the Devil**

  I have been binding the Devil every morning for more than fifty years. I was invited to speak at a youth camp in New York. The director had a Bible study every morning. One day he told this story:

  "I was in town and passed the camp doctor. He did not speak to me. I turned around, caught up with him and said, 'Is there something wrong?'

  "He said, 'Yes, you have a new camp doctor.'

  "'No,' I said. 'You are our camp doctor.'

  "'No, I know that you have a new doctor. Last year, you sent me 142 sick kids. This year you have sent only three sick kids. I know you have a new doctor.'

  "A light went on in my mind. At the beginning of the year, we started to bind the Devil every morning in detail. We bound him over all the camp activities, and only three kids had gotten sick."

  Now a light came on in my mind. If it will work for this camp, it will work for me back home in my family and in my business.

  How do you bind the Devil? I pray every morning something like this: "May the Lord rebuke you, and I bind you, all your helpers, all your demons and every means that you use. I command you in the name of Jesus. I command you to leave my four daughters, my four sons-in-law and all their children. I command you to leave the radio station alone, in the name of Jesus, the building, the equipment, the ministries, the employees and their children. I command you in the name of Jesus to leave the wood shop alone inside and outside and the sign."

Since I retired, I have a building where I manufacture furniture that is a front to win souls. I have a sign on the street that says, "Are you seeking peace in your life? The answer is in the Bible. Come inside, and I will give you a free Bible."

When people come inside and ask for a Bible, I say, "Come to my office, and I will give you a free Bible." In my office I say, "Do you have a minute?"

They generally say, "Yes."

I say, "Sit down." Then I start my plan on soul winning. I have seen approximately 130 people won to Christ.

Then I pray for the company and the radio station. "I command you, in the name of Jesus, to leave the property alone, the building alone, the equipment alone, the ministry and all the staff, their husbands or wives, their children, the ordering of new merchandise, the receiving of it, putting it away, picking new orders, the shipping, the payments, the advertising program, the catalogs, and all the details of the company, my home and all the contents." I continue on. "I bind you, Satan. I command you, in the name of Jesus, to leave the flags, the flag poles, the pump house, the sprinkling system, the heating system, the conveyors, the stock pickers, the high lifts, the welders, the customers, the catalog, the web machine, and I bind you, Satan, in the name of Jesus, to stay out of the company."

4. **Conduct Personal Devotions** — Spend one hour in prayer every morning:

    *   Worshipping the Lord.

    *   Confessing sin.

    *   Searching your heart.

- Being filled with the Spirit.
- Meeting your problems on your knees before you meet them during the day.

I was traveling and speaking in the early 1950s. One day I was traveling to Rochester, NY, to speak in a church. As I was entering Rochester, I was passing the Gerber Baby Food factory when the Lord spoke to me. It was so clear, "Stanley, if you don't give me the first hour of your day, you are not going to amount to much." I was afraid not to obey. For more than fifty years now I have given my first hour of the day to the Lord in prayer.

It has been a blessing and a ministry to meet my problems on my knees before I meet them during the day and to know I have already prayed about them. Besides this, my wife of 67 years and I have always had family devotions.

I stayed with a representative of the Family Altar. He told me that ninety-six percent of all Christian families do not have family devotions. What a blessing they are missing. If you are going to bear fruit, you must have a way to keep in shape. If a farmer is going to raise a crop, he first has to break up the soil. Praying Hyde was a missionary in India—born in Illinois. He had never seen so many people and had a burden for them. He asked God to win an average of one soul per day. Lo and behold, at the end of the year, he had led an average of one soul per day to Christ. His faith increased, and he asked God for two souls per day. Lo and behold, he had averaged two souls per day at the end of the year. His faith increased, and he asked God for three souls per day . . . then four souls per day . . . then five souls per day. He witnessed to a passenger on a train. He/She would come to his station but hadn't yet made a decision for Christ. He would stay on the train and travel until that person gave his/her heart to Christ. He would pray all night for souls. They said when he died that his heart had travelled from his left to his right side because he had prayed that much.

5. **Ask God for divine wisdom and knowledge to make decisions**—Do this every morning. It is a good feeling to know that you prayed about all the decisions that you will make all day. You have to make only fifty-one percent correct decisions to succeed.

- In the early days I lacked so many answers that I stayed up late in prayer, waiting for God to give me answers.

- When I have an important decision to make, I read the Bible until the Holy Spirit gives me Scripture for guidance.

- I keep myself in a state of "Thy will, not my will."

- Read the Bible every day to know God's will and thinking on subjects.

6. **Make a covenant with the Lord that every time you lose your temper or hurt somebody, you will apologize to that person.**

- *Whenever our hearts condemn us. For God is greater than our hearts, and he knows everything* (1 John 3:20).

- This is how you retain your testimony with people.

- God loves a broken and contrite heart.

- All great Christians are humble.

- An empty person is one filled with him- or herself.

This is one of the basic truths if you are going to have any power in your Christian life. I was speaking in a church in Atlanta, GA. Following the evening meeting, the pastor came to me and said, "My church was healed today." And then he explained about the altar service. "Did you see those two ladies on each side of the church meet in the center of the church and hug each other? My church has been divided for years by those two strong-willed Christians. A majority of the ladies has taken one side of these two ladies, but today the Holy Spirit unified them when they met in the middle and asked each one to forgive the other." Unforgiveness will rob you of your power with God quicker than any other thing.

I had an experience like this in the 1940s when I was a young Christian. (See also Chapter 15, pages 115-116.) The post office told us that if we were located in an area less than fifty percent built up, we would have to pick up our mail ourselves. At that time, we were receiving approximately 100 packages per day. Instead of going to the front of the post office, we had to go around back to the dock and ring a bell to get our mail. A man as slow as molasses would answer the bell by coming out to identify you. Then he disappeared for 15 minutes or so before he came out with the mail. One morning I was in a hurry. I rang the bell, he came out and he saw who I was. Fifteen minutes went by and no mail. I looked in the window and saw him fiddling around. All he had to do was write up the insured packages. A message began to stir in me, and when he did come out, I delivered it. I didn't swear, but the tone of my voice revealed that I was angry. I threw the packages in my pickup truck and left.

When I stopped at the street, the Lord said, "Stanley, are you a Christian?"

I said, "I know what you are going to bring up. I know that I lost my temper. I tell you, Lord, I will apologize to him tomorrow."

The next morning I went to the dock and rang the bell. Out he came with another man going across the street to the coffee shop on his break. Because he had company, I didn't apologize. I got my mail and left.

As I stopped for the street, the Lord said to me, "You didn't do what you promised me."

I said, "Lord, I will make a promise to you that I will keep. The next time I meet this man, regardless of the circumstances, I will apologize to him." Well, the man lost his job at the post office. I forgot all about the problem.

One day the pastor of the Second Baptist Church, a black church, called me and said, "I am going out of town on a certain date. Will you fill my pulpit?"

I agreed to do so. I got to this church just as Sunday school was letting out. Guess who the Sunday school superintendent was in this church? The man from the post office! I tried to get to him, but he avoided me. Pretty soon the morning service started. I sat on the platform with the layman in charge. As I was looking over the congregation, I spied the man in the center aisle about halfway down. The Lord said, "This is your opportunity to apologize to him."

I said, "Lord, not this morning. I am a guest speaker. This is the first time I've ever been in this church."

The Lord said, "You promised me."

I was in a spot. What shall I do? "All right, Lord. I will do it."

When I got up to speak, the man got up and walked out. Watching him, I said to myself, "I don't blame him. If I were him, I wouldn't want to listen to me either." But I reasoned, "Nobody in this congregation knows about our problem. I will continue with my message."

About halfway through, I had just said, "If you want power in your life, you have to have a clean life." The door opened, and in walked the Sunday school superintendent. He came back to the seat he had left and sat down.

The Lord said to me, "This is a good time to apologize to the superintendent."

I stopped speaking for a minute. Then I said, "I see your Sunday school superintendent has just come back in. I owe this man an apology. Would you excuse me while I give it?"

"Mr. Uptegrove, will you forgive me for the way I spoke to you at the post office? I am sorry."

You could have heard a pin drop as I apologized to their superintendent. I don't think I have had my hand shaken as much as it was that day after that service.

Apology did something for me. I don't think my automobile touched the pavement between the Second Baptist Church and my home. There was a revival going on in my heart. That apology also taught me not to tell off a person.

7. Get out of debt, and stay out of debt.

When you are out of debt and God speaks to you, you can obey because you are not shackled with debt. Three automobile sales companies asked an accountant for help in making more money. The accountant shared with them a way to pay for one car every few months so they would pay less in interest someday yet own the cars they sold. Two didn't take his advice, but one did. Several years later a mild depression hit the economy. Those two dealers are out of the car market. The one who followed the accountant's advice said he had the best year ever. He was able to purchase everything at a discount.

Being out of debt:

- Strengthens your marriage. Debt is the number-one cause of divorce.
- Enables you to take advantage of bargains and opportunities.
- Helps you sleep better at night.
- Allows you to become an example of one who depends on God.

8. Have a ministry of some kind so that you will grow spiritually in your Christian life.

- Lay up for yourself treasures in heaven.
- Responsibility keeps you tuned up spiritually in prayer and Bible study.
- It keeps you fresh spiritually.
- The work of the Lord gets done.

9. **To become an above-average Christian, share your faith.** Ninety-eight percent of all church members never win one soul in their lifetime.

- *You did not choose me, but I chose you and appointed you to go and bear fruit—fruit that will last* (John 15:16).
- *This is to my Father's glory, that you bear much fruit, showing yourselves to be my disciples* (John 15:8).
- God loves an obedient Christian.
- Paul said, "I am a debtor to all men."
- Win a soul to Christ.

My wife and I were coming home from Florida. Our plane was called, and everybody boarded. There was only one seat left, and it was beside me. They closed the door and were preparing to back out for departure. All of a sudden the door opened, and an elderly woman boarded. She was crying and took the seat next to me on the aisle. I leaned over and asked, "What's wrong?"

She was dressed well and nice looking. She said, "Speak up. I am hard of hearing." I repeated my question. Then she began to pour out her heart. "My daughter in Atlanta tried to commit suicide, and she is in the hospital. My husband is an invalid. I had to find someone to take care of him. I can't drive. I live twenty miles from the airport, and I had to find someone to drive me here. I don't know what to do when I get to Atlanta."

Everybody around us was listening, because she was talking

loudly. I said to her, "Lady, this is too heavy of a load for you to carry." (The Holy Spirit was speaking through me.) "I know somebody who can carry this load for you."

She looked at me and asked, "Who?"

I replied, "The Lord Jesus Christ. Do you want me to tell you some things about Him?"

She looked at me and said, "Yes."

I had to talk loudly, and everybody around us was listening. I began to tell her about the Lord Jesus Christ . . . why He came to this earth . . . how Adam and Eve had made all of us sinners . . . how Jesus' death on the cross paid for all of our sins if we would accept Him as our Lord and Savior. "Would you like to receive Him into your heart?"

She said, "Yes." She prayed and accepted Christ.

When we arrived in Atlanta, those who were seated near us said how glad they were that the lady sat with me. Two weeks later I received a letter from her thanking me for leading her to Christ.

Friend, always be ready to share your faith!

10. **Tithe your personal income**— *'Bring the whole tithe into the storehouse, that there may be food in my house. Test me in this,' says the Lord Almighty, 'and see if I will not throw open the floodgates of heaven and pour out so much blessing that you will not have room enough for it'* (Malachi 3:10).

- Lift this curse from yourself.
- This is the only money that you will keep from the time you live on earth.
- Become rich toward God.

- Be an example.
- Keep a set of books on how much you owe God.
- If you tithe your income for 10 years, you will have given one year of your annual salary.
- Pay your tithe to God or to the hospital.
- Don't have a curse on your life.

I was taught to tithe the day that I was converted. In 1934 I had $10 to tithe, and I had a church envelope. This is when money was worth considerably more. Soda pop was a nickel, a candy bar was a nickel, and an ice cream cone was a nickel. I put the envelope in my pocket and went to church. When the offering was taken, I reached into my pocket for my tithe envelope. It wasn't there. I went out to my car, and it wasn't there. I went home, and it wasn't there either. I said, "Lord, you will understand. I gave it to you in the envelope, but it just came up missing." That wasn't the end of it. My spirit struggled with that answer. I hadn't given the tithe money until it was in the church's hands.

Tithing is a command. It's the money we owe the Lord for the use of His property while we are on the earth. I don't want God's curse to be upon me.

(See also Chapter 8, pages 53-58.) One day I discovered that I was losing many of my customers on the east coast. Upon looking into it, I discovered that a company was manufacturing the very same silver collector that I was manufacturing, and they were recovering silver. I got excited. I wrote this company a letter telling them to stop manufacturing these silver collectors and that they were infringing on a patent. They didn't answer my letter, but a law firm did. They said they were representing the company in question and that they had studied the patent. They said the patent was so weak it wouldn't hold up in court. They advised their client to manufacture the silver collectors in question.

When I got that news, I wrote to Mr. Aukerman in Cleveland and told him the contents of the attorney's letter. I informed him that I wasn't going to pay him any more royalties because his patent was not enforceable. Mr. Aukerman sent his attorney to talk to me about the contract I had signed with him. I told him if the patent wasn't good, then the contract wasn't good. I stopped payments to Mr. Aukerman.

Several years passed, and the pastors of our city held a city-wide crusade. I was asked to have all the churches hold prayer meetings for the crusade. This was in 1952 when churches held a midweek prayer service. I was to present the needs of the crusade and ask the church to pray for them.

One night we were in a church and the pastor gave me time to present the need to pray for the city-wide crusade. He asked me to stay on the platform and close the meeting. We went to prayer. About halfway through, the Lord began to talk to me. "Why have you treated Mr. Aukerman and his patent the way you have?"

I replied, "We are praying for the crusade."

The Lord said, "I must talk to you about Mr. Aukerman and his patent."

I don't know what went on in that prayer meeting that night. I now had my own problem. I prayed about it for days. I discussed it with my wife who advised me to discuss it with Mr. Aukerman. Because he was quite elderly, he now lived in Wilmington, DE, with his daughter—about 600 miles from where I lived.

At the time World War II was happening, and many things were rationed. I couldn't get a plane ticket, but I finally got a train ticket. I stood for the first 200 miles before I finally got a seat. I rode all night until about 10 a.m. the next morning.

When I got to Wilmington, I called Mr. Aukerman, who was

expecting me. He and his daughter picked me up. Instead of taking me to their home, they drove downtown to a high building with a sign that said, "The Home of the E.I. DuPont Company."

Mr. Aukerman said, "We are going in here."

We took the elevator to the sixth floor, and they ushered me into a beautiful office with thick carpet, a walnut desk, and easy chairs. But when I was introduced to the first man—an accountant— and the second man—a corporate attorney—I felt like Daniel walking into the lions' den. I learned later that Mr. Aukerman's daughter worked for the attorney, and she had invited these two men for my visit.

The attorney reached into his desk, pulled out a letter and said, "We received this letter from you stating that you would like to meet with Mr. Aukerman. Could you tell us why you have come?"

I stood and said, "Yes, I would like to tell you. I have sinned against Mr. Aukerman by breaking my contract with him. I have come hoping that we can come to an agreement that is within my means to pay." I told them that when I was eighteen years old, I accepted Christ as my personal Savior and that I was struggling to live a successful Christian life. It was for this reason that I was there. They were surprised by my comments and were happy I had come.

We got down to business. They excused me and called me back into the room several times. Around 3 p.m. we came to an agreement: $500—within my means to pay. I agreed and signed the papers. This sum included the rights to the patent.

As I left to catch the train back to Lima, OH, I said, "Lord, I have obeyed you. I have made restitution. Will you seal this with a soul on the way back?" In a very unusual way the Lord gave me a soul.

Mr. Aukerman had said, "When you get home, we will send you some papers to sign. Please return them with a check for fifty percent of the amount you agreed to pay us. Then six months later, we expect the balance."

I received the papers, signed them and sent them back with the check. I sat back and thought, "It's all over but the second payment."

About six weeks later I got a letter from the accountant who had been in the room that day. When I opened it, I was shocked by the contents: "Mr. Aukerman died of a sudden heart attack. We buried him December 9."

What if I had not made restitution? When Mr. Aukerman goes before the Lord at the Great White Throne of Judgment to answer for his sins, he will never be able to say, "I stumbled over Mr. Tam going into hell regarding a business transaction."

Today his daughter professes to be a born-again Christian.

11. **Develop at least one testimony message**—If your testimony is a freight train, the locomotive is your subject, box cars are your experiences and the caboose is the decision. Each box car represents a new section of your testimony. This way you can have a short testimony or a long one.

- Expand your ministry. Start in a small group and then expand.
- Go to the rescue mission and practice speaking to groups.
- Develop a decision that you want people to make at the end of your talk.
- This gives you a tool to win souls to Christ.

12. **Maintain a spiritual diary**—When an interesting spiritual

experience happens to you, write it in your diary. When you have enough, write a book.

- Hire a professional writer to write your book if you need help.

- Your diary will remind you that God answered prayer once; He will do it again.

- Your diary gives you a source for material that you might otherwise have forgotten.

- Your diary encourages you to keep going.

13. **Make goals in your Christian life** — in giving, winning souls, etc. Work to see them come to pass. Have a professional company produce a video on your operation, incorporating your spiritual story. Make it available to other businesses, churches, class meetings, men's meetings, etc. Having goals keeps you tuned spiritually. For example, your goals might include:

- Win three souls per day for twenty-three years.

- Speak to one million people about Christ.

- Trust Him for $xx for church and missionary work.

- **One of My Goals**

    In 1952 on our speaking trip around the world, the most important thing I saw was the OMS Every Community for Christ (ECC) ministry in Japan. The OMS ECC employed nationals and formed them into teams of six men each. They had seven teams covering the country of Japan. They had already covered the entire country, every home on every island with the gospel of John, and they were winning souls to Christ.

    They were covering the country the second time, having tent meetings in the evening for men who worked during the day. I couldn't forget this ministry. In 1968 OMS ran out of money and had to shut down this ministry. I was led by the Lord to approach the president of OMS. I asked that if I could trust the Lord for $50,000, would they be able to start up the ECC again. They agreed. Today—forty-four years later—the ECC is in forty-four countries, and there are 146 teams. In 2012 these teams reported over 1 million decisions for Christ. The budget is $5 million per year. United States Plastics Corp.® has given their earnings to this ministry and still have to raise $1-2 million.

14. Have a prayer partner—Meet once a week to pray about your businesses.

- Eighty-three percent of our prayers were answered affirmatively.
- Conduct Bible classes for the unsaved—to date, 101 decisions.
- Added Gospel tract racks—up to twenty-two.
- Started Christian radio station.
- Pray for the unsaved.
- Pray about each other's business.

About twenty years ago, an Inter-Varsity representative visiting in my office asked a strange question.

"Mr. Tam, do you have any friends?"

"I have a lot of friends," I answered.

"Do you have one true friend?"

"What do you mean?"

"Well, suppose you fell into sin or went into bankruptcy or an accident left you a hopeless cripple, do you have a friend who would stick with you through thick and thin?"

"No-o-o," I replied slowly. "I guess I don't have a friend like that."

"Mr. Tam, there is a movement going across our country in which men like you have a prayer partner. And ladies, too, have a prayer partner. You would meet at least once a week and pray together for each other."

Then he proceeded to explain the philosophy behind the idea.

"Every Christian has a weak side. You have a weak side. That is where Satan always attacks. But if you have a prayer partner, your weakness will probably be his strength. The Bible speaks about one chasing a thousand and two putting ten thousand to flight. When you have a prayer partner, you become ten times stronger!"

It sounded logical.

"If you read the Word of God," my friend continued, "you will find prayer partners all the way through the Scriptures. Moses had Aaron, David had Jonathan, Paul had Silas. Christ did not send out His disciples one by one. Had He done so, all of them might have returned defeated. He sent them out two by two, and they returned victorious, saying, 'Even the devils are subject unto us.' The Scriptures also say, *Again, I tell you that if two of you on earth agree about anything you ask for, it will be done for you by my Father in heaven"* (Matthew 18:19).

My Inter-Varsity friend so challenged me that I telephoned a business friend.

"Art," I said, "I must have lunch with you today. I have something to talk to you about." During lunch I explained the whole proposal and asked him if he would be willing to be my prayer partner.

"Tam," he replied, "I believe this is of God. I will make a covenant with you for one year." It is a covenant that we have renewed year after year for 38 years.

We meet on Thursdays at the city park in his automobile or mine, where no telephone can interrupt our prayer time. I pray for Art. Art prays for me. I pray for his business. He prays for mine. I pray for his family. He prays for mine.

There in the city park, God put it upon our hearts to ask Him for a ministry. In the Lord's leading we began a Bible class at the plant I manage. It was a neutral place where the unsaved were not reluctant to come and study the Word of God. During the years we have seen more than 100 people come to know Christ as we studied the Word with them and talked to them about Jesus Christ.

15. **Prepare a piece of literature** to include in your shipments, giving your testimony. This gives you a tool to win souls. For example:

- Print it on the back of an article (e.g., how to take spots out of your carpet).

- Put your testimony on the back of your company's money guarantee folder.

- Leave it with a tip at restaurants or filling stations.

- When someone asks for your calling card, give him/her a copy of your testimony.

In 1938 I called a photo finisher in Chicago. When I walked into his business, I saw a table loaded with thousands of Gospel tracts. When I met the owner, I said, "What do you do with all these Gospel tracts?"

He replied, "We are in the direct-mail photo-finishing business, and we put one in every roll of film that we process. Our customers read them."

I said, "If you can do it, we can do it."

We have been putting Gospel tracts in every shipment of plastic products for seventy-three years. Last year we made approximately 250,000 shipments. About twenty-five of our customers write to us each month to say they have accepted Christ as their personal Savior. I write to each one with a letter of instruction about how to grow in their born-again experience. I send them a copy of my book. Then we enroll them in the Navigators Bible study material.

This is using your business as a pulpit. There are other ways you can make your business a pulpit.

16. **Build a reputation with God**—Be a person upon whom God can depend. Obey when God speaks to you. Then God will use you.

   * God said of David, *I have found David son of Jesse a man after my own heart; he will do everything I want him to do* (Acts 13:22).

   * Two voices—Which one do you obey?

   * Don't let God down. When you accept an assignment, keep it.

   * Always keep your word. When you promise to be there, be there.

Remember, God likes and will use Christians who keep their word, upon whom He can depend and those who are obedient to Him.

17. **Become rich toward God**—Begin to lay up treasures in heaven by giving Him twenty percent, thirty percent, forty percent, fifty percent of your net profits. If you are going to heaven, you need to deposit funds in the bank of heaven. This is the only money that you will ever keep.

   * Keep a spiritual bank account.

   * Ask yourself, "How rich do I want to be in Heaven?"

   * Your business tithe is different from your salaried tithe. Your business tithe is figured on your profit after all expenses are paid. Normal profit in a business is five percent to twelve percent. Tithe on this.

The Bible doesn't command us to give any part of our business to the Lord. It is a step of wisdom. It is part of Jesus saying, "Lay up for yourself treasures in heaven."

We cannot evangelize the world with the tithes of the average Christian. It takes large sums of money, and only with the gifts of businesses can we evangelize the world. In fact, we need still more money.

God is pleased with anybody who gives beyond his/her tithe.

18. **Ask God for a spiritual project** to fully or partially support, such as building a church on the mission field.

- Support a group such as Every Community for Christ.
- Drill water wells for the nationals.
- Support a missionary.
- Support a national seminary student.
- Supply the literature for a certain field.
- Write a book like *God Owns My Business*.

The command is *Go into all the world and preach the good news to all creation* (Mark 16:15). The problem is that there aren't enough Christians who will sacrifice and give support to missionaries so they can take the Gospel to the ends of the world. Another great need is prayer for the lost. Christians who could give of themselves to pray for the souls of the world are without excuse.

In 1940 my heart was filled with gratitude toward God for making my business a success to the point that my wife and I had decided to make God our senior partner in our little business. We went to a lawyer and said, "We want to make God our senior partner."

The lawyer incorporated our business and established a foundation, and we turned fifty-one percent of the stock over to this foundation. While we were in South America in 1955, God told me that He wanted the entire business. That year we gave the entire business to God.

19. **Print your testimony** in business to pass out. Let your customers know that you are a Christian. Let them know why you are a Christian and how to become one. It's a door opener when you meet a friend or stranger. Print your testimony:

- To leave in a restaurant with a tip.
- To leave in a store when you make a purchase.
- With your address for when someone asks for your calling card.

I don't believe I could be a successful witness for Christ unless I have my testimony printed. It makes it so easy to share your faith with your printed testimony. When you sit down on an airplane, you can politely strike up a conversation with the person next to you. Soon he or she will ask what kind of work you do. Reach in your pocket, pull out your testimony and say, "This is my story. Read it." Then sit back and pray while he or she reads it. When he or she has finished reading your story, say, "Would you like to receive Christ as your Savior?" About one-fourth will say, "Yes."

When you eat in a restaurant, leave a copy of your testimony with a generous tip. I generally write on the top of my testimony, "Thank you for being a good server to me." Then the server will know that I didn't forget it when I left and that it really was for him/her.

When you purchase something, say to the clerk, "If I give you my story, will you read it?" Ninety-nine percent will say, "Yes."

One day I received $20 in the mail. It was from a server in New York City. With it was a note saying, "Thank you for the compliment at the top of your article."

Here is a suggestion: Begin with a story (if you have one) of how you were almost killed—get your audience's attention. Then explain your conversion experience. Give no more than five passages of Scripture throughout your testimony. Remember, all of this is new to them.

20. **Identify your business with God** by hanging a picture of Christ in your lobby or by some other way, such as hanging a "Christ Is the Answer" sign outside on your building.

- You are an epistle read by all men.

- People will know to whom they can go for spiritual help.

- It encourages other Christians to know that you are not afraid to witness for Christ.

- It is obedience to God's commands—let your light shine.

21. **Thank God for every adverse event in your life.**

- You wouldn't buy a car without Reverse on it.

- The greatest blessing in the world is sickness. It keeps us closer to God.

- When my doctor said I had cancer, I said, "Thank you for cancer." It gave me a tool to encourage other Christians.

- Adverse events remove tension in your life.

- **The Power in a Christian**

   I began speaking engagements in 1942. In those days we traveled by train. I received an invitation to Kingston, NY, and traveled on a train that went through New York City and proceeded north along the Hudson River.

Suddenly the door of my car opened and in walked guys whom I described as thugs.

I was seated near the front of the car. Nobody was in front of me. They stopped where I was seated and pulled out a deck of cards. They made a row of cards in front of me and commanded me to pick one card.

I looked at the men and said, "In the name of Jesus Christ, pick up your cards and leave." Their eyes grew large, they looked at one another and they picked up their cards and left. I was as surprised as they were to my command in the name of Jesus Christ. That experience has never left me—the power of God through me.

Dr. Loveit, a great man of God who was involved in one of the translations of the Bible, told of this experience in *Binding the Devil*. He lived in the residential area of Los Angeles. Being a man of God, he put a printing press in his basement and began printing Gospel tracts as a hobby.

As time went on, his hobby grew and he now had several printing presses in his basement. Several people also worked for him each day printing the Gospel tracts. His unsaved, pessimistic neighbor was endlessly annoyed with the cars parked in front of his house every day. One day this man called the city and reported his neighbor who had a business going on in his basement in a restricted area of the city. The city stopped Dr. Loveit from printing tracts in his home business. Dr. Loveit felt so badly that he couldn't sleep night after night.

One night he read about "binding the Devil." He read that you have to talk out loud because the Devil is not omnipresent. This night he went into the bathroom where he could shut the door and talk out loud. He bound Satan and went back to bed and slept the rest of the night.

For our struggle is not against flesh and blood, but against the rulers, against the authorities, against the powers of this dark world and against the spiritual forces of evil in the heavenly realms (Ephesians 6:12).

22. We advance by our reverses.

- If I hadn't been fired at a filling station, I might not have gone into business.

- Reverses make us stronger Christians.

- Reverses give us victorious testimonies.

In 1936 I started a business reclaiming silver from photographic film. I believe it is the world's toughest business. It took a photographer about nine months to accumulate a pound of silver on one of our silver collectors. At $.35 per ounce, this amounted to only about $5.60. We would split the silver: fifty percent for the photographer, fifty percent for the company. It was the Lord who made us succeed in this business.

We were in this business for about ten years when we heard there was a tax on silver. I had been selling my silver to a refinery in Chicago. I thought I had better find another place to sell the silver. I chose a company in Connecticut who said they would be glad to buy our silver. On the first shipment, however, they wrote and asked for the paperwork for the tax on the silver for the U.S. government.

I replied that I didn't know about any tax on silver. They sent me a booklet called Government Regulation No. 84. (See also Chapter 9.) It said if you didn't pay the tax, you would owe the government fifty percent of the silver value, but if you paid, the tax the charge was ten percent.

The silver refinery in Chicago assumed I was taking care of the tax at my end and never questioned it. I prayed about it.

One day I got the courage and went down to the local IRS

office. I told them about my trouble. I was sent to Toledo, OH, to the miscellaneous tax division. The man referred to a huge book and said, "The book says there is a silver tax, but I don't know what to do with you. You have operated for ten years without paying the tax. I will have to send your case to Washington, D.C., for them to decide."

Washington, D.C., wrote and asked what the volume of silver was that I was processing. I figured out that I owed the government $23,000. At that time in 1946, $23,000 was enough to retire on and live happily ever after. I couldn't pay $23,000! I went home from the office that evening, took a nap and waited for my family to go to bed. Then I labored in prayer. I told the Lord that I would like to work in a factory where I could go home at night with no further obligations. I complained and complained some more when the Lord spoke to me.

He said, "The problem is that you have sin in your life—a bad sin. Do you know why you have problems in your life? You have sin in your life."

"What kind of sin? Is it adultery, drinking, swearing?"

"No, it is worse than these. It is unbelief. If you will get rid of that sin, I will take care of your problem. It is as simple as that."

That night I got through to the Lord. I cast my unbelief on the Lord. I went to bed and slept through the night.

You say, "It's Christian psychology???"

No, it's like our silver. It has impurities in it, but we know we can put the silver in a crucible and turn the heat up to 2,300°F. All the impurities will come to the top, and we can skim off the impurities and pour a pure bar of silver. If we would put the silver in the crucible, turn up the heat and the silver started to complain, saying, "It's too hot in here! Get me out! Get me out!" and we took it out soon after we put it in, it wouldn't do any good.

That's what God does. He looks at us, sees our impurities and says, "That person needs some refining." So He puts us into His crucible and turns up the heat. We begin to holler. If He took us out as soon as He put us into His crucible, it wouldn't do us any good.

A year went by when I received a letter from the government saying, "We forgive you of all of the tax you owe except $447." I had the $447, so I was glad to send that amount.

Life is like an oyster. When a grain of sand gets into an oyster, what does the oyster do with the grain of sand? Does he complain about it? No, he begins to build something with it—a beautiful pearl. When a reverse comes into your life, don't complain about it. Take it to the Lord and thank Him for it. Ask Him to build something beautiful out of it.

Distribute 60 Copies of this Book and Likely Win Someone to Christ

God Owns My Business already has a long publishing history. To date 450,000 copies have been printed in several languages. Many people have come to faith in Christ, re-dedicated their lives, or changed their business practices as a result of this book.

Perhaps you would like to share the book with friends or colleagues. We sincerely believe that the prayerful distribution of 60 books is likely to produce at least one sincere decision for Christ. For this reason we have created the "Caring Christian Discount of 50%" if you will buy one case of 60 books for such distribution.

Just fill out the form below and mail it to:

United States Plastic Corp.®
1390 Neubrecht Road
Lima, OH 45801

Or call (419) 228-2242 or FAX (419) 228-5034 or order online at www.usplastic.com and use stock number 1002.

Please clip and mail

Please send your check along with your name and address to United States Plastic Corp., 1390 Neubrecht Road, Lima, Ohio 45801.

Name: _____

Address: _____

City:_____Zip: _____

Please send me _____ case(s) of *God Owns My Business.*

I enclosed herewith $190.00 for each case ordered.

(60 books at $6.00 each, less 50% equals $180.00. Please add $10.00 for postage and handling on each case, total, $190.00 per case of 60 books.)